THE EUCHARIST IN
BIBLE AND LITURGY

THE EUCHARIST IN BIBLE AND LITURGY

The Moorhouse Lectures 1975

G. D. KILPATRICK

CAMBRIDGE UNIVERSITY PRESS

Cambridge
London   New York   New Rochelle
Melbourne   Sydney

Published by the Press Syndicate of the University of Cambridge
The Pitt Building, Trumpington Street, Cambridge CB2 1RP
32 East 57th Street, New York, NY 10022, USA
296 Beaconsfield Parade, Middle Park, Melbourne 3206, Australia

First published 1983

Printed in Great Britain by
New Western Printing Ltd, Bristol

Library of Congress catalogue card number: 83–14315

British Library cataloguing in publication data
Kilpatrick, G. D.
The Eucharist in Bible and liturgy. – (The
Moorhouse lectures; 1975)
1. Lord's Supper
I. Title   II. Series
264′.36   BV825.2

ISBN 0 521 24675 X

WP

CONTENTS

PREFACE

First, I thank all concerned for the invitation to deliver the Moorhouse Lectures in Melbourne, Australia, and secondly, all who have asked me to give parts of these lectures in other places, in particular the Bishop of British Columbia in Victoria B.C. I am grateful for comments and suggestions made in many places and by many friends.

The literature on the topic is immense and much that I would have liked to study further has gone unremarked. As it is, I owe an apology to all concerned for the delay in presenting these lectures for publication.

Certain themes have been touched on in my early book, *Remaking the Liturgy* (Collins, 1967), but liturgical studies and revisions have moved since then and the careful reader may notice differences between the two books. I have sought to remove a number of features which were more appropriate to the original lecture form of the theme and apologise for any elements which ought to have been corrected.

For New Testament books I use the following abbreviations: Mt., Mk., L., J., A., R., 1C., 2C., G., Ph. (Philippians), C., 1T. (1 Timothy), H., Rv. A variant reading in the passage cited is indicated by '*v.l.*'

Finally I must acknowledge the patience and helpfulness of officers of the Cambridge University Press.

G. D. KILPATRICK

LECTURE I

❦

The background
The New Testament accounts: (1) Mark xiv
                              (2) Matthew xxvi
A note on the text of Mark xiv.22–5 and Matthew xxvi.26–7

Differences in words and the ideas behind them separate us from the world in which the Eucharist came into being. Part of my exploration will be directed to these differences.

We must be prepared to find that words and ideas which are central for us in this connexion are alien to the Biblical world, and Biblical words and ideas prove strange to us the more we examine them.

Let us take two examples and, first, one of a word with its ideas which is now a commonplace of Christian doctrine, but was unknown in that connexion in first-century Christianity, the word 'sacrament'.

A sacrament is described as 'an outward and visible sign of an inward and spiritual grace' in the Catechism of the English Book of Common Prayer. This or similar descriptions have been current among Western Christians for nearly 1600 years. St Augustine at the end of the fourth century A.D. seems first to have used the word with this kind of meaning. First-century Christians had neither the word 'sacrament' nor the corresponding description. I do not know of any word in the original Greek of the New Testament that can be translated in this way, nor will you find it even in the Authorised Version of the Bible, sympathetic as the makers of this version may be held to be to the idea. Sacrament and the meaning we associate with the word are foreign to the world of the Bible.

Our second example is 'sacrifice', the word and the institution. It is still current in ordinary English and in Christian theology, but I doubt whether in either it has its Biblical meaning.

Some years ago I saw in a shop window during a sale a frock at a reduced price described as a sacrifice. This would have sorely puzzled an ancient Israelite and I still cannot guess what he would have made of it, so far has the word departed from its Biblical meaning.

If we were to ask an ordinary believing Christian what the word 'sacrifice' means for him, we might find that he associated it with two notions, first, the notion of atonement through suffering and, secondly, the notion of vicarious suffering or death, to suffer or die instead of another. Such an answer would show how far our Christian of today is from the reality of sacrifice. In fact death can be sacrificial, but there is nothing about vicarious death that makes it sacrificial. If it is sacrificial, it is not because it is vicarious. If by contrast we look at the various sacrifices recorded in the Old Testament, we see that most of them are meaningless to us, though they were full of significance to the men of the Old Testament, who developed and maintained an elaborate system of sacrifice which could only be justified if it was concerned with things that mattered for them.

I shall later on return to these words, 'sacrament' and 'sacrifice', to treat them in more detail, but I trust that you are now alerted to the fact that we are dealing almost with two distinct religious languages. We often use them as though they were one and the same, but we shall be forced more and more to recognise their differences, that on the one side sacrament is a word foreign to the Bible, and that on the other sacrifice and the institution of sacrifice are foreign to us today.

Nor are these the only such words. Later I hope to show that the word 'holy' has quite different meanings for us and for the men of the Bible and that there are considerable differences between the main Biblical use of 'bless' and our use of the term today.

If, in moving into the Bible, we are alert to the fact that we are entering a new world with languages, ideas and institutions so strange to us and are leaving behind some of the familiar notions we have grown up with, we must not overlook that we and the men of the Bible have a great heritage in common.

It is a good thing to be made aware of these conditions of our common exploration of the Eucharist. They force us to try to think carefully and precisely about what we want to say and, if we meet differences of opinion, to state as exactly as we can what those differences are.

Let us take an example. Inevitably in my treatment of the Eucharist I shall examine the chief New Testament passages which deal with it, three in the Gospels and one in 1 Corinthians. What is our attitude in this connexion to the New Testament and the Bible as a whole? I see the Bible as the collection of the foundation documents of our religion and a principal vehicle of the Word of God.

You may say: why does he not say straightforwardly that the Bible is, or is not, the Word of God? Why all this hedging? To this I reply that I am concerned to say no more than the Bible says. The Bible claims more than once to carry the word of God, but never identifies itself with the Word of God. Indeed I have been told that the identification of the Bible as it stands with the Word of God was not made before the time of

St Augustine. I have never checked this statement, but the identification of the Bible as a whole with the Word of God without qualification has always seemed to me an innovation.

There is another qualification which we must notice. We live in an age of printing, though it is not clear how long we shall continue to do so. I have in front of me a copy of the New Testament in the second edition of 1970 of the New English Bible. All copies of this issue of the New Testament will have the same text. Indeed we can generalise this and say that all copies of the same issue of the same book have the same text unless they are damaged. We are so used to this state of affairs that we do not readily imagine a time when it was different.

Yet there was such a time. Before the age of printing, books were copied word for word by hand, and we can say at once that no two copies of the same book had the same text throughout, and for two reasons.

First, if you start copying a text from a book by hand you will notice that after a time you begin to make mistakes and, if you go on copying, you make more mistakes. You will not be the first to do so. Even professional copyists made mistakes, some more than others, but none were faultless.

Secondly, scribes made deliberate changes. Stated baldly this may sound more shocking than the making of mistakes, but it was a process which affected books copied by hand, and the surprising thing would have been if it had failed to happen, especially if the book were at all popular.

Some forty years ago I wrote a paper on certain aspects of the Gospels and sent it to be typed. In the paper I referred to the theory of the composition of Luke known as Proto-Luke. The typist apparently had never heard of Proto-Luke; she decided it was a mistake and looked round for an expression that seemed to make sense and decided that Protestant Luke was what was wanted, and so, when I read through the typescript, Protestant Luke was what I found.

Let me give another example. Just now I mentioned the New English Bible. I was a member of its panel for the New Testament and was involved in at least one other translation. This led me to study the making and revision of Biblical translations. I noticed that one kind of revision consisted in the modernisation of language.

Here is an example. In the original text of the Authorised Version of 1611 you will find a number of times the word 'moe', but 'moe' later went out of use and the word 'more' was substituted for it. We find 'more' in the eighteenth-century and later printings. In the Authorised Version of today I shall be surprised if you will find any examples of 'moe' left.

This is a trivial instance and many of the changes that scribes made in the text of the Bible were trivial too, but now and then alterations of greater significance were made. Some of them we shall have to consider later on.

One further point we should consider. I have mentioned the variations of our manuscripts. Can it be that among their variations at some points in our Bible the original form of our text has been lost and can be recovered only by guesswork? In principle this is possible, but in practice I find it very unlikely in the New Testament. As far as the New Testament is concerned, it seems that we can rely on finding the original form of the text at each point in some or other of our witnesses despite their variations.

If we have to allow for the accidents that may happen to a book over centuries of copying by hand, we have also to allow for another handicap in dealing with our texts, the fact that they are written in another language. Many people in North America, for example, grow up without encountering any language other than English and find it hard to imagine the reality of another language. Often in their efforts to do so they imagine the other language as just being English in another form, thanks to the perversity of foreigners.

In this way they assume that the other language will be unambiguous where English is unambiguous and will share its ambiguities. For instance the English sentence 'Drink ye all of it' (Mt. xxvi.27) is ambiguous. Does it mean 'All of you, drink of it' or 'Drink the whole of it'? We can debate this endlessly as long as we confine ourselves to the English version but, as soon as we look at the Greek, ambiguity is at an end. Thanks to certain features in the structure of New Testament Greek which are not shared by modern English, the Greek sentence can only mean: 'All of you drink of it.'

Sometimes words have a narrower range of meaning in one language than in the other. We discover, for example, that the Greek words for 'poor', 'rich' have a wider connotation in the Greek New Testament than their accepted English equivalents.

Earlier I mentioned the four passages in the New Testament reporting the institution of the Eucharist (Mt. xxvi.26–9, Mk. xiv.22–5, L. xxii.15–19, 1C. xi.23–5). I shall have in this and the next two lectures to discuss these accounts against a background of assumptions about the tradition about Jesus as a whole.

What are these assumptions? In attempting to answer this question I shall consider, first, characteristics which are not peculiar to the tradition and, secondly, characteristics which are.

Let me illustrate the first characteristics. When I was an undergraduate in Oxford in the 1930s, the Group Movement was active there. I attended a number of its meetings, where it was customary for members of the Group to speak. Part of what they said consisted of stories. Each member had his story of how he was brought into the Groups, how he was 'changed'. He had also a number of stories illustrating the Groups and their leading members.

The story of how he was changed had a clearly defined structure. First, it gave a picture of the member before he was changed. Naturally this picture was in sombre colours. Then the incident when he came into contact with the Groups and was 'changed' was reported. Finally he told, as far as modesty would allow, how much happier and how much better he was since he had joined the Groups. Invariably each member's story of how he was 'changed' tended to conform to this pattern.

Besides his own story each member had the stories which he acquired through his membership of the Groups. He was encouraged to learn such stories off by heart so that he could relate them spontaneously at Group meetings for interested outsiders.

He was also encouraged to write down these stories in his notebook, the first stage in the written, as distinct from the oral, tradition of such material. These stories began to constitute small collections which themselves grew in size and sometimes were systematically arranged. Some of them formed the core of chapters in books. In this way in the course of a few years this body of material made the passage from the single story told orally to the printed book.

The tradition about Jesus experienced in many ways a comparable development. We can still detect the single story, the collection of stories or other material, and finally the written work.

There are, however, characteristics that are peculiar: the tradition about Jesus underwent two migrations. To start with, the tradition about Jesus seems to have existed in oral form in Aramaic. It seems at a relatively early stage to have made the migration from Aramaic to Greek. The suggestion that the earliest form of the tradition in Aramaic was oral need not surprise us. There are many examples of oral tradition in Judaism. For instance, most of the Talmud was handed down in oral form before it was written.

When the tradition migrated into Greek, conditions were different. Oral tradition was not unknown in the Greek world, but normally, when a Greek wished to put forward an idea or a philosophy, or other teaching, sooner or later he wrote a book. Indeed philosophers were among the first writers of books in Ancient Greece. As soon as the tradition about Jesus entered into the Greek world, there seems to have been pressure to put it into writing, first of all in collections of increasing size and then in books, our empirical Gospels.

This order of migration corresponds with the lack of clear traces of Aramaic documents, as distinct from Aramaic oral forms, in the tradition about Jesus. Had the two migrations taken place in the reverse order, the migration from oral to written before the migration from Aramaic to Greek, we would have expected to find traces of Aramaic documents.

Though it does not come into my discussion, let me here mention the document Q, hypothetical as it is. I regard this hypothesis, despite recent arguments to the contrary, as being the best explanation of certain features of the tradition. Before the composition of Q, the migration from Aramaic to Greek had already been made. Its Greek seems to have been on a higher level of style than that of Mark and John. Fortunately Q, as we shall see, affects my investigation little.

Earlier I mentioned the three chief passages about the Eucharist in the Gospels. I must now report my view of the relationship between Matthew, Mark and Luke. Mark, on this view, is the oldest, and was used as the source for much of their material by Matthew and Luke, who are independent of each other. Though they both seem to have used other sources in other parts of their Gospels, I shall argue that in their accounts of the Institution of the Last Supper they used only Mark.

This should cause little difficulty where Matthew is concerned. I shall notice two significant differences from Mark in Matthew's account, but otherwise Matthew contributes nothing distinctive and important.

When I contend that Luke had only Mark as his source for the Institution Narrative, I enter much more controversial country. One of my tasks will be to explain and defend this conclusion. If I am right, we shall find Luke more instructive about the Eucharist in the early Church, if less informative about origins.

For full measure let me confess that John seems to me to have known and used Mark. Scholars in recent years have put forward hypotheses of varying complexity which avoid this conclusion. I sometimes wonder whether some of them were designed to this end. The issue will prove of some relevance when we discuss J. vi.

These statements of opinion about the Gospels imply that there are two primary accounts of the Institution at the Last Supper, Mark's account and that in 1 Corinthians. 1 Corinthians is the older but Mark, unlike 1 Corinthians, is presented to us as a solid piece of tradition and for that reason will be considered first.

What do we know about Mark? Various dates have been proposed for Mark but about A.D. 65, a few years before the Fall of Jerusalem in A.D. 70, seems to me most likely. The raw material of his Greek is on a lower level than that of Matthew and Luke, and implies a man who had little education as that was understood in the Graeco-Roman world of his time. He could read and write, but had no training as a writer. On the same level stand John, Revelation and, surprisingly, the Pastoral Epistles.

Socially and economically the conditions implied by the Gospel would agree with this. Much of Palestine was a poor and backward part of the Roman Empire. The largest sum of money mentioned in Mark is 300 denarii, as much as a farm worker might earn in a year, when farm workers were paid a subsistence wage. Social contacts mentioned in the Gospel would agree with this. Mark is in complete contrast in all these features with Luke, who shows pretensions to literary education and many of whose characters belong to a higher and wealthier level of society.

On the other hand we must not undervalue Mark. If our evangelist is lacking in education in Greek terms he came from a province which had its own Biblical and Jewish culture, of which he shows an awareness. He has natural gifts as a writer and uses Greek with clarity, sensitiveness and strength. He does not often present us with the awkwardness of thought and language that we meet in Luke.

The impress of Semitic idiom is strong on his Greek. Whether he depended immediately on written or oral sources, the stage when the tradition about Jesus was in Aramaic lies not far behind our evangelist. He still has some expressions in Aramaic.

The account of the Institution of the Eucharist in Mk. xiv.22–5 reads as follows:

And while they were eating he took bread, said a blessing and broke it and was giving it to them and said, 'Take, eat; this is my body.' And he took the cup and gave thanks and gave it to them and they all drank of it. And he said to them, 'This is my blood of the covenant which is shed for many. Verily I say to you that I shall not again drink of the fruit of the vine until that day when I drink it new in the kingdom of God.'

This differs very little in substance from the translation you know. At one or two places I have translated a Greek text a little different from the text commonly printed, but you have now been warned that this might happen.

'Bless' is one of the words that need explanation. We use it freely, but do we know what it means? In origin it seems to be a pagan English word and clearly meant 'mark or smear with blood' or the like. At the conversion of the English it was christianised and is now used as we know.

We do not know the original meaning of the Semitic *barak*, which is current both in Hebrew and Aramaic, but it appears to signify 'give power, vigour, strength' to someone or something.

This 'someone or something' raises an important point. We are used to maintaining a clear distinction between God and man, between people and things, but in primitive times it was not so. The difference between God and man is blurred and, more surprising, that between God and things seems to fade away.

You remember the story of Jacob's dream at Bethel on his way to stay with Laban in Mesopotamia (Genesis xxviii). He put a stone for a pillow under his head, went to sleep on it, dreamed his dream, and in the morning took the stone which he had put under his head and set it up for a *massebah* and poured oil on the top of it and said: 'This stone which I have set up for a *massebah* shall be God's house.' All very well, but why does he pour oil on it? Oil is used to convey life and strength. He does not want to give these just to a stone but as an offering to his God, but in practice he does not distinguish.

In the course of the Old Testament this distinction is made rigorous. 'Bless' is confirmed more and more to God and men in its application and in the New Testament is rigorously so restricted. The few apparent exceptions that we find prove on examination to be only apparent.

The same is true in Rabbinic Judaism. The tractate *Berakoth* ('Blessings') in the *Mishnah* contains material from the first two Christian centuries and not later. In it we have a number of blessings in their actual wording. Unlike many Christian blessings they have an exclusive Godward direction. We say: 'Bless, O Lord, these thy gifts.' Rabbinic Judaism said and says over bread: 'Blessed art thou, O Lord our God, King of the Universe, who bringest forth bread from the earth', and over wine: 'Blessed art thou, O Lord our God, King of the universe, who createst the fruit of the vine.'

Early Christianity was in line with Jewish practice in this matter. For example, Judaism has a grace after meals, the *Birkath ha-Mazon*, of which the first two paragraphs now run as follows:

Blessed art thou, O Lord our God, King of the universe, who feedest the whole world with thy goodness, with grace, with loving kindness and tender mercy; thou givest food to all flesh, for thy lovingkindness endureth for ever. Through thy great goodness food hath never failed us: O may it not fail us for ever and ever for thy great name's sake, since thou nourishest and sustainest all beings, and doest good unto all, and providest food for all thy creatures whom thou hast created. Blessed art thou, O Lord, who givest food unto all.

We thank thee, O Lord our God, because thou didst give as an heritage unto our fathers a desirable, good and ample land, and because thou didst bring us forth, O Lord our God, from the land of Egypt, and didst deliver us from the house of bondage; as well as for thy covenant which thou hast sealed in our flesh, thy Law which thou hast taught us, thy statutes which thou hast made known unto us, the life, grace and lovingkindness which thou hast bestowed upon us, and for the food wherewith thou dost constantly feed and sustain us on every day, in every season, at every hour.

By good fortune we have from the fourth century A.D. three Christian cousins of this prayer. The first comes from a handbook of Christian practice of the second half of the fourth century (the *Apostolic Constitutions* VII.xlix) which begins: 'Blessed art thou, Lord.' The second form is found in Ps.-Athanasius, *De Virginitate* xii which also seems to belong to the fourth century and has nearly the same text as the *Apostolic Constitutions*.

The third form, which is quoted in Chrysostom's commentary on Matthew a few years later, is fuller (PG lviii.561):

Blessed art thou, God, who dost feed us from our youth and dost give food to all flesh; fill our hearts with joy and gladness that we always have enough of everything and may abound to every good work in Christ Jesus our Lord, with whom glory and honour and might be to thee with the Holy Spirit for ever, Amen. Glory be to thee, Lord, glory to thee, holy one, glory to thee, O king, because thou hast given us food for rejoicing. Fill us with the Holy Spirit that we may be found well-pleasing before thee and may not be put to shame when thou requitest each man according to his works.

The earlier part of this prayer down to 'Amen' is used as the grace at dinner at Oriel College, Oxford.

Earlier I mentioned apparent exceptions in the New Testament. 1C. x.16, for instance, is rendered 'the cup of blessing which we bless'. An examination of New Testament usage suggests that the rendering should be 'the cup of blessing as to which we say the blessing', the blessing being not the blessing of the cup but the blessing of God said over the cup.

Similar is the use of the word for 'thanksgiving' (*eucharistia*). In the New Testament it is used for giving thanks to God. Later in the ancient Church it is transferred to the elements and writers describe them as being 'Eucharistised'. How does this come about?

We may find something of an answer to this question when we look at the history of the words for 'bless' in the ancient Church. εὐλογεῖν, the Greek word for 'bless', meant 'to speak well of, to praise'. Only when it is used to translate the Hebrew *barak* does it come to mean 'bless'. In the Greek Bible it shares in the increasing limitation of this word to God and mankind. In the ancient Church its use widens to include the blessings of things and we find it used in Origen and the liturgies from the fourth century for blessing the Eucharistic elements. The Latin *benedicere* has a parallel history in pagan usage, meaning 'to speak well of, to praise'. Next it shares the limitation of εὐλογεῖν and Hebrew *barak*, expanding its meaning in the Latin Church to include things. In the fourth century and subsequent liturgical texts it is used of blessing the Eucharistic elements. A valuable piece of research would be the exploration of this widening of the meaning of Greek εὐλογεῖν and Latin *benedicere* in Christian use until they reach the sense of 'bless' or 'consecrate'.

'Covenant' requires comment but this had best be deferred until I treat of sacrifice. Unlike the use of the word now, when its associations are principally legal, covenant in the Bible is in terms of sacrifice.

After Mark we can treat Matthew's account very briefly. Earlier I discussed the relation of Matthew's account to that of Mark. If I may repeat, Matthew takes over Mark with only two significant changes. First Mark has 'And he took the cup and gave thanks and gave it to them and they all drank of it.' Matthew changes the last clause to direct speech 'and gave it to them saying: "All of you drink of it." ' This change brings the text on the cup into line with that on the bread, 'Take, eat', and is an instance of the tendency to conform the two parts of the narrative into line with each other.

The second change will prove later on to be more significant. After the words over the cup 'shed for many' Matthew adds 'for the forgiveness of sins'. We may regard this as a perfectly legitimate expansion of the story, but, as we shall see later, it may have an interesting bearing on the early history of the Eucharist.

A note on the text of Mark xiv.22-5 and Matthew xxvi.26-7

The following changes are proposed in the text of the BFBS edition of 1958 (= Nestle Aland[25]). The reading of 1958 is put first and then, preceded by a square bracket, the proposed reading.

Mk. xiv.22 λαβών] + τόν M Σ 69–983–1689 22 348 713 *al*. The article is often used in the New Testament in a way recalling Hebrew idiom, cf. M. Black, *An Aramaic Approach to the Gospels and Acts*[3] (The Clarendon Press, 1967), pp. 93ff. Jeremias' protest, quoted by Black on p. 93, seems justified; cf. Mk. i.13 οἱ ἄγγελοι, L. xviii.2 *v.l.* ἐν τῇ πόλει, and my article 'Jesus, his Family and his Disciples' in the *Journal of New Testament Studies*, XV (1982), 3–19. The same interpretation would apply to verse 23 τὸ ποτήριον 'the cup' in this incident.

εὐλογήσας] εὐλόγησεν καὶ D 50 *L* a d. Parataxis is frequently changed to hypotaxis, a participle and a main verb instead of two main verbs joined by καί, as a matter of style, cf. H. J. Cadbury, *The Style and*

Literary Method of Luke (Harvard University Press, 1920), pp. 134f. All the other New Testament accounts have a participle.

ἔδωκεν] ἐδίδου W f1 f13 495 1542. For the change from imperfect to aorist see W.C. Allen, *The Gospel According to St. Matthew*, International Critical Commentary (T. and T. Clark, 1912), pp. xxff and Cadbury, *The Style and Literary Method of Luke*, p. 160.

εἶπεν] + αὐτοῖσ W Δ Θ 299 565 *L* i k *S* s p *C* b(2). In the interests of Greek style in contrast to Semitic style, it is common to omit pronouns, especially forms of αὐτόν.

λάβετε] + φάγετε E F H S V Ω M² X Y Γ Σ *0116* f13 28 157 Ω. φάγετε is usually regarded as an assimilation to Mt. xxvi.26, but the shorter text can be explained as the product of ὁμ., λαβΕΤΕφαγΕΤΕ.

23 λαβών] + τό A K Y Π P W Γ Φ Ω. See above on τὸν ἄρτον.

24 ὑπέρ] περί A K Y Π Σ Φ *0116* Ω. ὑπέρ with the genitive occurs only at ix.40 for certain in Mark. περί recurs in Mark some thirteen times. This agrees with the general tendency for περί with the genitive to be used instead of ὑπέρ.

25 πίω] προσθῶ πιεῖν D (πιειν) Θ 565 *L* a f Arm. This reading reproduces a Semitic idiom; see J. Jeremias, *The Eucharistic Words of Jesus* (S.C.M. Press, 1966), pp. 182f, and V. Taylor, *The Gospel According to St. Mark* (Macmillan, 1955), *ad loc.*

Mt. xxvi.26 We may read τὸν ἄρτον and verse 27 τὸ ποτήριον as in Mark, and we may be uncertain about the variation in verse 26 δοὺσ.. εἶπεν] ἐδίδου.. καὶ εἶπεν, but otherwise Matthew's text seems to present no problems.

The changes in Mark's text do not seem to affect the substance of the narrative (and this is even truer of Matthew), but they do heighten the colouring of Semitic idiom, justifying Jeremias' contention (Jeremias, *The Eucharistic Words of Jesus*, p. 173).

LECTURE II

❧

The New Testament accounts: (3) 1 Corinthians xi
(4) comparison of Mark and
1 Corinthians

Let us now turn to the other principal account of the Institution, 1C. xi.23–6. It may be translated in this way:

For I received from the Lord what I have also handed over to you, that the Lord Jesus in the night in which he was handed over to custody took bread and when he had given thanks he broke it and said, 'This is my body which is for you; do this for my *anamnesis*.' In the same way the cup also after the meal saying, 'This cup is the new covenant in my blood; do this as often as you drink it for my *anamnesis*.' For as often as you eat this bread and drink this cup you proclaim the Lord's death until he comes.

In this translation I have left the word *anamnesis* untranslated because its meaning is debated and it seemed better to discuss what it signifies before we give a rendering.

'Memory, remembrance, memorial' are normal meanings of the word and properly come to mind as translations of it here. Further, the traditional and customary equivalents in other languages have assumed for it this kind of significance, and, if this were all, we would readily translate the word in this way.

However there are three difficulties in this interpretation. First, it ignores the Apostle's own explanation, 'you proclaim the Lord's death until he comes'. Here it is proclamation and not memory or remembrance which is significant. This leads to the second difficulty. As we explore the background and the origins of the Eucharist we shall find that the idea of memory plays little or no part in it. The third difficulty is that while the word *anamnesis* has various meanings in the dictionaries, this interpretation does not rest on a discussion of them.

A second interpretation occurs in Dom Gregory Dix's book, *The Shape of the Liturgy* (Dacre Press, 1945), p. 245:

First, we have to take account of the clear understanding then general in a largely Greek-speaking church of the word *anamnesis* as meaning a 're-calling' or 're-presenting' of a thing in such a way that it is not so much regarded as being 'absent', as itself *presently operative* by its effects. This is a sense which the

Latin *memoria* and its cognates do not adequately translate, and which the English words 'recall' and 'represent' will hardly bear without explanation, still less such words as 'memorial' or 'remembrance'.

Though Dix's view has become fashionable in some quarters, it is difficult to find evidence for it. Indeed we may suspect that its attractiveness rests on the fact that it enables us to read into the text an idea that we want to find there. I can see in the use of the word no evidence that it can properly bear this meaning. It may be implied in the context, but that is another matter.

Professor J. Jeremias has advanced a third interpretation in his book, *The Eucharistic Words of Jesus*, pp. 237–55. He quotes passages from the ancient Greek versions of the Old Testament which have the meaning 'remember and help'. We can see how this may come about. 'Do this for my *anamnesis*' might be paraphrased 'Do this in order that God may remember me and act' and the more precisely 'that God may succour me'. This interpretation is much better substantiated than that of Dix.

Nonetheless, it has its difficulties. First, it too ignores the Apostle's remark 'you proclaim the Lord's death until he comes'. Second, we shall have to consider the authenticity of the remark, and Jeremias' interpretation may prove unhelpful here. Third, the rest of the story stresses much more what has been accomplished than what is hoped for. This is true for example in the explanation, 'you proclaim the Lord's death', a past event, not a wish for the future.

The Apostle's explanation should give us a hint of the correct interpretation, 'proclamation', but I have not been able to find any example of this meaning for *anamnesis* itself. If this were all, I would be in no better plight than Dix.

There is one consideration that may make this lack of evidence a little less surprising. The study of the vocabulary of the New Testament has in the last century owed much to the discovery and exploration of papyri from Egypt, as can be seen from such works as J. H. Moulton and G. Milligan, *The Vocabulary of the Greek Testament* (Hodder and Stoughton, 1930), and Preisigke and Kiesseling. This material however comes largely from Egypt and we have no finds of papyri from Antioch.

I am assured that the spoken Arabic of Beirut differs noticeably from the spoken Arabic of Cairo. We may infer from this that in the first century A.D. the spoken Greek of Antioch differed from the spoken Greek of Alexandria. We can only infer this because of our lack of evidence from Antioch. Inscriptions do not help us here as much as papyri would, as the language of inscriptions is as a rule much more formal and shows much less local variety.

The Acts of the Apostles seems to be right in representing the early Christians as moving from Jerusalem to the North rather than the South (A. xi .19–21, 26f), to Antioch rather than Alexandria. Indeed we lack any solid evidence for an organised Christian Church in Alexandria before the middle of the second century A.D.

With this we may link the fact that we find in the New Testament terms which cannot be paralleled from Egyptian papyri of the first century. Apart from ἐπιούσιοσ in the Lord's Prayer, which was otherwise unknown to the Egyptian Origen, we may instance such terms from the Epistles as δυνατῶ (R. xiv.4, 2C. ix.8, xii.10 *v.l.*, xiii.3), ἀνεβαλόμην (G. ii.2 F G), and ὀρθοποδοῦσιν (G. ii.14). In the same way, we have to allow that ἀνάμνησισ 'proclamation' may have been not unknown at Antioch. This is a speculative suggestion, but it enables us to meet the contention that had ἀνάμνησισ this sense we would have had other extant evidence for it. In this connexion it is important to establish the meaning of καταγγέλλειν as precisely as we can, as giving us a clue to the meaning of ἀνάμνησισ.

καταγγέλλειν and its compound προκαταγγέλλειν occur only in Acts and the Pauline Epistles, in all some twenty times. These are enough to determine its content.

καταγγέλλειν
(1) ὁ λόγοσ τοῦ θεοῦ, τοῦ κυρίου A. xiii.5, xv.36, xvii.13
τὸ εὐαγγέλιον 1C. ix.14
ὁδὸσ σωτηρίασ A. xvi.17
φῶσ A. xxvi.23 (God's salvation)
τὸ μυστήριον τοῦ θεοῦ 1C. ii.1 *v.l.* μαρτύριον
(2) ὁ χριστόσ A.xvii.3, Ph. i.17, 18, C. i.28
ὁ θάνατοσ τοῦ κυρίου 1C. xi.26
ἡ ἀνάστασισ A. iv.2
ἄφεσισ ἁμαρτιῶν A. xiii.38
τὰσ ἡμέρασ ταύτασ A. iii.24 (the prophet like Moses = Christ)
ἄγνωστοσ θεόσ A. xvii.23 (God and Christ)
(3) ἔθη A. xvi.21 (Christianity)
πίστισ R. i.8 (the faithfulness of the Romans to Christian teaching)

προκαταγγέλλειν
παθεῖν τὸν χριστὸν αὐτοῦ A. iii.18
περὶ τῆσ ἐλεύσεωσ τοῦ δικαίου A. vii.52

From this we can see that the content of καταγγέλλειν is always religious even at R. i.8, explicitly the Christian dispensation. The first group of instances centres on the proclamation of the Word of God, the second group on the Messiah. This would encourage us to understand εἰσ τὴν ἐμὴν ἀνάμνησιν as meaning 'to proclaim one as the Messiah' or the like, but the Apostle narrows the content to the death of the Messiah. Here we remember that verse 26 gives us the Apostle's interpretation, and when he limits the content of the ἀνάμνησισ to the death of Jesus he is interpreting it much too narrowly. Hippolytus, in his Eucharistic Prayer, adds references to the Incarnation and our salvation and the ancient Church followed him in this. We may well think that they were right, but the Apostle has set us on the right track by using καταγγέλλειν, the verb of proclamation, with a religious content as the explanation of ἀνάμνησισ.

This is not all. The Greek verb corresponding to the noun ἀνάμνησισ is ἀναμιμνήσκω, and in it we find what we want. Let us look at some examples:

(i) Exodus xxiii.13 'You shall not proclaim (ἀναμνήσεσθε) the name of other gods nor shall it be heard from your mouth.' The counterpart to the verb 'be heard', ἀκουσθῇ, in the second clause is 'tell, proclaim', which suggests that our translation is correct. The point is not that the Israelites shall fail to remember the name Chemosh for the god of Moab, but that they shall not proclaim it.

(ii) Amos vi.10 'Silence, we may not name the name of the Lord.' Here the later Greek translators, Theodotion, Aquila and Symmachus, of the first and second centuries A.D., have our verb ἀναμνῆσαι, this time meaning 'utter, speak', an interpretation supported by the command 'silence', which would be irrelevant if the reference was to memory.

(iii) Psalm xlv.17 (xliv.18) 'I shall proclaim (ἀναμνήσω) your name in each generation: therefore peoples shall praise you continuously for ever.' So the three translators, Theodotion, Aquila and Symmachus, render the passage. The point is not that the psalmist goes on reminding himself from one generation to another, but that he tells successive generations. As the next line shows, this is followed by praise from nations, an unlikely consequence of an internal act of memory.

There are one or two debatable instances elsewhere in the Greek Old Testament but these are enough to establish this usage there, cp. Brown, Driver and Briggs, *Hebrew and English Lexicon*, 270b–271a.

In the New Testament there are perhaps two instances of this meaning.

(i) 2C. vii.14f 'as all that we told you was true so also our boasting about Titus proved to be the truth and his affections went out to you more abundantly as he told (ἀναμιμνησκομένου) of the obedience of all of you, how you received him with fear and trembling'.

The meaning 'told' is at least as likely as the meaning 'remembered' in view of the references in the context to telling and boasting.

(ii) 2T. i.6 'I tell you (ἀναμιμνήσκω) to revive the gift of God.' It is questionable whether more than 'tell' is meant though 'remind' is possible.

Now let us look again at *anamnesis*. I have argued that in some passages of the Greek Bible the corresponding verb seems to mean 'tell, proclaim', and in others may have this meaning. We may go on to infer the corresponding meaning 'proclamation' for the noun. This agrees with what the Apostle wrote: '"Do this as often as you drink it to proclaim me." For as often as you eat this bread and drink this cup you proclaim the Lord's death until he comes.' On this showing, the *anamnesis* or proclamation of Jesus is interpreted as the proclaiming of his death and the stress is not on remembrance but on this proclaiming.

Is this proclamation confined to telling the death of Jesus only? The Apostle himself implies that it includes his coming again. Perhaps we can go further and infer that it contained the kind of brief account of the Institution that we find in Mark and 1 Corinthians.

Before we ask what other acts may have been part of the proclamation, let us consider where it may have taken place in the course of the service. Earlier we saw that the blessing of God, the thanksgiving to him at meals, could be quite lengthy. The customary form as it now stands gives thanks for supplying all mankind with food, for giving Israel its land, for the deliverance from Egypt and for the Covenant and Law. It would not surprise us to find that the thanksgiving, the blessing of God at the first-century Eucharist, had a similar character, retailing God's saving acts and his provision for all mankind.

To come to this from the other end, we may ask what can the early Christians have said at the thanksgiving? It is not enough to quote the Rabbinic blessings of the bread and the cup which I have mentioned earlier. We have no evidence to suggest that they used them, nor do they provide for the proclamation that the Apostle mentions. We would expect them to say something more like the Jewish grace mentioned earlier, with a text appropriate to the occasion.

We have a clue to the contents of the thanksgiving from a later time. Some 150 years after the writing of 1 Corinthians, Hippolytus, the Roman theologian, wrote his liturgical handbook, the *Apostolic Tradition*. In it he gives a pattern for the Eucharistic Prayer as follows:

We give thee thanks, O God, through thy beloved servant whom thou hast sent to us in the last times as saviour and redeemer and herald of thy will, who is thine inseparable word through whom thou madest all things, who was well-pleasing to thee, and whom thou didst send into the virgin's womb; conceived within her he was made flesh and was shown forth as thy son born of the Holy Spirit and the virgin; he fulfilled thy will and won for thee a holy people, stretching out his hands when he suffered to deliver from suffering those who trusted in thee; when he was delivered to voluntary suffering to destroy death, break the chains of the Adversary, tread down Hell, enlighten the righteous, establish the decree and show forth his resurrection, he took bread and gave thanks to thee and said: 'Take, eat, this is my body which is broken for you.' In the same way the cup also, saying: 'This is my blood which is shed for you. As often as you do this you make my *anamnesis*.' Making therefore the *anamnesis* of his death and resurrection we offer thee this bread and this cup, giving thee thanks that thou hast judged us worthy to stand before thee and to serve thee as priests.

You may have found this thanksgiving not only tedious (other men's thanksgivings often are tedious) but also obscure. You are not alone in this and the reason is not hard to find. Hippolytus wrote in Rome in Greek and little of the Greek text has come down to us. All we have are Latin and Oriental translations, and so the text that I have quoted is a translation of a translation. Hence at least some of the obscurities.

The part of the prayer which I have quoted consists of a thanksgiving for the saving acts of the Lord beginning with the Incarnation and ending with the Resurrection. It is the oldest specimen of Eucharistic Prayer that we have, but the fourth-century prayers have the same core. The *Apostolic Constitutions* (VIII.xii.38) adds at the end a reference to the Ascension and the Second Coming but apart from such details the pattern remains the same.

From this we can see that certainly two and perhaps all three of the items I inferred from 1 Corinthians are present in Hippolytus' prayer, the Institution Narrative, the death and perhaps the Second Coming. To that extent we can regard the later Eucharistic Prayer as being in line with Pauline practice. For the *Birkath-ha-Mazon* we may refer to J. T. Talley's instructive treatment, *Worship*, L (1976), 115–37.

If we compare this with the *Birkath-ha-Mazon*, which I quoted in the first lecture, we notice certain contacts. These are the deliverance of God's people and the making of a covenant. In the Christian liturgy these references are in terms of Christ, in the Jewish prayer to the deliverance from Egypt and the Covenant of circumcision.

In the *Didache*, which in its present form was perhaps composed about A.D. 160, we have some thanksgiving texts which have been cited as examples of the Eucharistic Prayer. They run as follows:

And concerning the thanksgiving give thanks thus: First concerning the cup, 'We give thanks to thee, our Father, for the holy vine of David thy child, which thou didst make known to us through Jesus thy child; to thee be glory for ever.' And concerning the breaking: 'We give thee thanks, our Father, for the life and knowledge which thou didst make known to us through Jesus thy child. To thee be glory for ever. As this broken bread was scattered upon the mountains, but was brought together and became one, so let thy Church be gathered together from the ends of the earth into thy kingdom, for thine is the glory and the power through Jesus Christ for ever' (*Didache* ix.1–4).

But after you are satisfied with food, thus give thanks: 'We give thanks to thee, O Holy Father, for thy Holy Name which thou didst make to tabernacle in our hearts, and for the knowledge and faith and immortality which thou didst make known to us through Jesus thy child. To thee be glory for ever. Thou, Lord Almighty, didst create all things for thy Name's sake, and didst give food and drink to men for their enjoyment, that they might give thanks to thee, but us hast thou blessed with spiritual food and drink and eternal light through thy child. Above all we give thanks to thee for that thou art mighty. To thee be glory for ever. Remember, Lord, thy Church, to deliver it from all evil and to make it perfect in thy love, and gather it together in its holiness from the four winds to thy kingdom which thou hast prepared for it. For thine is the power and the glory for ever. Let grace come and let this world pass away. Hosannah to the God of David. If any man be holy, let him come! if any man be not, let him repent: Maran atha, Amen.' But suffer the prophets to give thanks as they will (*Didache* x.1–7).

It is tempting to see these prayers as Eucharistic, but there are the following difficulties.

First, in the Eucharist the order is bread and cup: here it is cup and then bread. It has been suggested that we have this divergent order in the shorter text in L. xxii also and on this basis scholars have argued that in these two texts we have an alternative Eucharistic tradition where cup preceded bread. Later I shall argue that this is to misinterpret L. xxii and that there is no such alternative tradition. On this matter of order the observance in the *Didache* is out of line with the Eucharist.

Secondly there is another difference in the order of the meal. If we follow the indications of 1C. xi, bread is broken and partaken with thanksgiving in the meal itself and a cup again with thanksgiving at the end. In the *Didache* first a cup is partaken with thanksgiving and then bread is broken and partaken and finally thanks are given for the meal. This last thanksgiving has contacts with the *Birkath-ha-Mazon*, with its references to spiritual goods as well as to food. The texts in the *Didache* look much more like the thanksgiving at a Jewish meal.

Thirdly the references to Jesus are peripheral and can be removed from the text without damaging its structure and content. Like the Eucharistic Prayer, the thanksgivings in the *Didache* are directed to God the Father, but, as we have seen, the core of the Eucharistic Prayer is the saving acts of Jesus and the Institution Narrative is recited. This is not true of the prayers in the *Didache*.

Fourthly the Eucharist is dealt with later in the *Didache* (xiv). We may notice in passing that in this later passage the Eucharist is described as a sacrifice. There is nothing corresponding to this in the earlier chapters.

We may now ask why some scholars have been inclined to regard these prayers as Eucharistic. Probably they did this because of the Christological references in the three thanksgivings. These references, however, are in keeping in any Christian prayer, and the absence of the declaratory words which are to be found in the other early accounts known to us prevents us from maintaining that more is involved than the use of a series of Christological themes. Their language contains Biblical echoes but this does not make them Eucharistic.

At the end of the thanksgiving over the bread comes the prohibition: 'But let none eat or drink of your thanksgiving except those who have been baptised in the Lord's name. For concerning this also the Lord said, "Give not that which is holy to the dogs" ' (*Didache* ix.5). It may be argued that this states the restriction of participation in the Eucharist to baptised Christians.

Against this contention we may recall the difficulties which showed themselves over the sharing in meals by Jewish and Gentile Christians in the first-century Church. Some Jewish members found it difficult to sit down to a meal with believing Gentiles. This is what happened at Antioch:

When Kephas came to Antioch I withstood him to his face because he was condemned. For before some came from James he used to eat with the Gentiles, but when they came he drew back and separated himself, fearing the men of the circumcision. The remaining Jews also played the hypocrite with him so that Barnabas too was carried away with their hypocrisy (G. ii.11–13).

If the early Church found it so difficult in practice to have meals in common within itself we can imagine how far early Christians would be from having their meals in common with the heathen.

We can see the background of ideas to this in 1T. iv.4–5: 'for everything that God has created is good and nothing that is taken with thanksgiving is to be rejected. For it is sanctified through God's word and prayer.' The meal that is made holy by thanksgiving cannot be shared with heathen. 'Give not that which is holy to the dogs.' We shall return to this text in another connexion.

If these considerations are relevant, then the exclusiveness of the occasion for which the *Didache* provides these thanksgivings is no reason for thinking that it was a Eucharist. It need be no more than an ordinary Christian meal.

Granted that the thanksgivings in the *Didache* ix–x are for meals in general and not for the Eucharist, we cannot find in them an alternative to the saving acts of the Lord which seem to form the main part of the Eucharistic Prayer. In this case we are left with the suggestion that already in 1 Corinthians we have the beginnings of the pattern of the saving acts that we know in more developed form in Hippolytus and the later liturgies. More precisely, ἀνάμνησισ means 'proclamation' and already in 1 Corinthians it is the proclamation of at least some of the saving acts.

This suggestion encounters one difficulty. In the later liturgies there is one proclamation of the saving acts in one prayer of thanksgiving, but in the accounts in Mark and 1 Corinthians there are two, one over the bread and one over the cup. How was the proclamation associated with these two distinct acts?

We have one hint at an answer to this question. Already in Paul's account we have a repetition. At the breaking of the bread we have the statement 'Do this to proclaim me', and over the cup 'Do this, as often as you drink it, to proclaim me.' This may suggest that in the two thanksgivings in the Pauline account there was a certain parallelism and overlapping. We may surmise that each thanksgiving contained the relevant part of the Institution Narrative, together with the command to repeat, as well as other of the saving acts. This possibility may seem easier when we remember that the action over the bread takes place in 1 Corinthians in the meal, but the action over the cup after the meal (μετὰ τὸ δειπνῆσαι 'after having had supper'). There is an interval between the two.

We notice in Hippolytus' prayer some duplications: 'saviour and redeemer', 'whom thou didst send into the virgin's womb; conceived within her he was made flesh and was shown forth as thy son born of the Holy Spirit and the virgin', 'when he suffered to deliver from suffering those who trusted in thee; when he was delivered to voluntary suffering to destroy death'. Is it possible that such redundancies may survive from a time when there were two thanksgivings which at least to some extent were saying the same or similar things? I should, perhaps, modify my hypothesis to propose two thanksgiving prayers rather than one, but my suggestion about the content would remain.

Perhaps I can go further than this. If we compare the accounts in Mark and 1 Corinthians, we notice differences of substance, like the presence of the two commands to repeat in 1 Corinthians which we have been discussing. We notice also certain differences in style when we look at the Greek. These differences can be informative. First there are the connecting words like 'and', 'but', 'for'. Such words are commoner in Greek than in English. Mark has either no connecting word, the practice called asyndeton, or else 'and'. 1 Corinthians has asyndeton, 'and', and 'for'.

Next, the adjective can be placed before or after its noun. In English the adjective usually comes before, in Greek it can come before or after, in Hebrew it comes after. In Mark we have one example only and there the adjective comes after its noun: τῆσ ἡμέρασ ἐκείνησ, but in English 'that day'. In 1 Corinthians we have four such phrases and in all the adjective comes first: τὴν ἐμὴν ἀνάμνησιν 'my proclamation' (twice), τῷ ἐμῷ αἵματι 'my blood', τοῦτο τὸ ποτήριον 'this cup', ἡ καινὴ διαθήκη 'the new covenant'.

In English, genitives come before the noun on which they depend: 'God's house', 'man's nature'; but in Greek they can come before or after and in Hebrew and Aramaic they come after. In Mark they always come after: τό σῶμά μου but in English 'my body', τὸ αἷμά μου but 'my blood', τοῦ γενήματοσ τοῦ ἀμπέλου 'fruit of the vine', τῇ βασιλείᾳ τοῦ θεοῦ 'the kingdom of God'. In 1 Corinthians we have only τοῦτό μού ἐστιν τὸ σῶμα 'this is my body', where the genitive μου 'my' is well ahead of its noun τὸ σῶμα.

In English the verb usually comes in the middle of its clause: 'the Queen visited Mexico', where 'visited' is in the middle. In Hebrew the verb more commonly comes at the beginning and this is still true to a large extent in Aramaic, as though we were to say 'came the Queen to Mexico', but in Greek there is much more variety. In Mark the verbs come most often at the beginning in their clauses or phrases: ἐσθιόντων αὐτῶν, λαβὼν ἄρτον, ἐδίδου αὐτοῖσ, λαβὼν ποτήριον, ἔδωκεν αὐτοῖσ, ἔπιον ἐξ αὐτοῦ πάντεσ, εἶπεν αὐτοῖσ, ἐκχυννόμενον ὑπὲρ πολλῶν. In οὐ μὴ προσθῶ πεῖν the negatives must come first. Further we have two examples of τοῦτό ἐστιν and one surprisingly enough of αὐτὸ πίνω. In 1 Corinthians we have no examples of the verb at the beginning of its clause or phrase. We have several instances of it in the middle: ἐγὼ γὰρ παρέλαβον, ὃ καὶ παρέδωκα ὑμῖν, ὁ κύριοσ . . . ἔλαβεν ἄρτον, τοῦτό μου ἐστιν, τοῦτο ποιεῖτε etc.

What do these details of style tell us? First, Mark's heavy reliance on 'and' is not literary Greek, but corresponds to usage in Hebrew and Aramaic. Secondly, in its placing of its adjectives 1 Corinthians is far removed from the idiom of Hebrew and Aramaic. Thirdly, in the placing of genitives Mark follows the grammar of these two languages, while 1 Corinthians does not. The same is true about the placing of the verbs. In all four features 1 Corinthians is contrasted with Mark. Mark is consistently near Semitic idiom and 1 Corinthians is further away.

As far as Mark is concerned, this fits in with what was said in the last chapter, where we noticed that 'the impress of Semitic idiom is strong on his Greek'. This is understandable. The tradition about Jesus was originally current in Aramaic. Subsequently it migrated into Greek and only when it was in Greek did it pass from oral to written, finally being incorporated in our Gospels.

Most of the material of this tradition was catechetical, used in the instruction of converts, rather than homiletic. According to the evidence available, the early Christian sermon made relatively sparing use of the details of the tradition about Jesus. They had been imparted more fully to those under instruction. To judge from the Gospels, this catechetical tradition stubbornly retained the traces of Semitic idiom, down to the final stages. We can see this quite clearly in our English Gospels and even more clearly in their original Greek. The expression 'answered and said' that we frequently meet in the Gospels in the Authorised Version is not English, nor can its Greek rendering be Greek. The expression is at home in Hebrew.

Mark, then, in the Semitic features of his Greek, is preserving something which goes back in the tradition as far as we can trace it. This suggests that in its greater distance from Semitic idiom it is the account in 1 Corinthians which has moved away from the earlier forms. Its Greek is more in keeping with normal Greek of the time.

This should mean that the Greek of 1 Corinthians is the product of a revision. As we have seen, the tradition about Jesus has to a remarkable extent avoided the elimination of Semitic features and this tradition was probably used catechetically. This being so, the revision of the Greek seen in 1 Corinthians is not likely to be for catechetical reasons.

It does not seem to be the work of Paul himself. He was not averse from retaining Semitic features. For example, he talks at R. i.4 of 'the spirit of holiness', where he means the Holy Spirit, using a more Semitic cast of expression. We may infer that the language of the account had already been conformed to normal Greek standards before it was quoted by the Apostle.

We have here a problem. The introductory words of 1C. xi.23, 'For I received from the Lord what I have also handed over to you', would lead us to expect a careful report of the tradition as Paul had received it. If we may combine this with G. i.18 ἱστορῆσαι Κηφᾶν, which we should translate 'get information from Peter' (cf. G. D. Kilpatrick, 'Galatians 1:18 ICTOPHCAI ΚΗΦΑΝ', in *New Testament Essays, Studies in Memory of T. W. Manson*, ed. A. S. B. Higgins (Manchester University Press, 1959), pp. 144–9), we may claim that 1C. xi.23–5 represents early tradition indeed.

This claim would conflict with the inferences that we have already made that, in contrast to Mark's account, the text of 1C. xi shows signs of revision, the reduction of emphasis on blood, the avoidance of Semitic idiom and an approach to a more normal Greek. How can the suggestion of revision be reconciled with such strong claims for the Corinthian passage?

Two features in this passage to which we shall return suggest that it does not represent the Apostle's own view of the matter. First, 1C. xi.25 runs τοῦτο τὸ ποτήριον ἡ καινὴ διαθήκη ἐστὶν ἐν τῷ ἐμῷ αἵματι against Mk. xiv.24 τοῦτό ἐστιν τὸ αἷμά μου τῆσ διαθήκησ, but we have noticed passages in 1 Corinthians which seem to reflect not the wording of 1C.xi.25, but the wording of Mark.

For example, 1C. x.16 τὸ ποτήριον τῆσ εὐλογίασ ὃ εὐλογοῦμεν, οὐχὶ κοινωνία ἐστὶν τοῦ αἵματοσ τοῦ χριστοῦ 'the cup of blessing as to which we say the blessing is it not a sharing in Christ's blood?' seems to imply the words of Mark τοῦτό ἐστιν τὸ αἷμά μου. Similarly 1C. xi.27 ὥστε ὃσ ἂν ἐσθίῃ τὸν ἄρτον ἢ πίνῃ τὸ ποτήριον τοῦ κυρίου ἀναξίωσ, ἔνοχοσ ἔσται τοῦ σώματοσ καὶ τοῦ αἵματοσ τοῦ κυρίου is much closer to Mark than to the more evasive words of 1C. xi.25.

A second feature lies in the word εὐλογεῖν 'say the blessing'. It comes in Mk. xiv.22 and, probably following Mark, in Mt. xxvi.26, whereas L. xxii.19 has εὐχαριστήσασ. As we have seen, Paul uses εὐλογεῖν at 1C. x.16 of the Last Supper whereas the narrative at 1C. xi.23–6 has εὐχαριστεῖν once and εὐλογεῖν not at all.

How are these differences to be explained? If we may assume that behind the Apostle's words lie two accounts we have the following picture: on the one hand the Apostle was influenced by an account of which we see traces in 1C. x.16 and xi.27, an account which would seem to be nearer the account we have in Mark; on the other hand we have the authoritative account in 1C. xi.23–6, which seems to be the product of a revision.

Why was the revision made? One possibility occurs to us. The account is of an institution that quickly became liturgical. Already in 1 Corinthians it contains the command to repeat: 'Do this to proclaim me.' We may go on to suggest that the account in 1 Corinthians is derived from liturgical use. This could explain the elimination of traces of Semitic idiom and the normalisation of the Greek.

This explanation would require that the Corinthian account reached its present stylistic form in a church which was definitely Greek-speaking and likely to serve the Apostle as a model of practice. This suggests a church in the Levant or Cilicia, and Antioch seems the most likely candidate. We may infer that the Apostle derived his account from the liturgical practice of Antioch.

If the mere attention to details of language and style can lead us, in a comparison of the accounts in Mark and 1 Corinthians, to the suggestion that Paul reports the narrative that was used liturgically at Antioch, let us see what an examination of the substantial differences between the two accounts will yield.

First, we have already noticed one such difference. 1 Corinthians has the double command to repeat that Mark lacks, 'Do this to proclaim me' and 'Do this, as often as you drink it, to proclaim me.' Has this double command been added in the tradition behind 1 Corinthians or has it been omitted in that contained in Mark?

In any case Jesus seems to have intended the repetition of the observance. Unless we argue that the covenant mentioned in the two accounts was only with those present, we have to suppose that there would be repetitions of the observance for other believers. To that extent the commands to repeat represent the intention of Jesus.

We ought perhaps to notice here a suggestion that the mention of covenant is an intrusion, a suggestion perhaps best known from earlier editions of Jeremias' work on the Last Supper, *Die Abendmahlsworte Jesu*[2] (Vandenhoeck und Ruprecht, 1949). Jeremias later recanted this suggestion (*The Eucharistic Words of Jesus*, pp. 193–5) for sufficient reasons, though we may think that more weight should be given to J. A. Emerton's article, 'The Aramaic Underlying τὸ αἷμά μου τῆσ διαθήκησ in Mk. xiv.24', *JTS*, VI (1955), 238–40. He has shown that the construction of a noun with a pronominal suffix followed by another noun in the genitive is possible in a Semitic language. He produced examples especially from the Syriac in support of this. We may also recall that both Mark and 1 Corinthians with all their variation have a reference to the covenant. Even Luke, who, as we shall see, handles the tradition more drastically, probably has a reference to the covenant at xxii.29 κἀγὼ διατίθεμαι ὑμῖν διαθήκην καθὼσ διέθετό μοι ὁ πατήρ μου βασιλείαν ἵνα ἔσθητε καὶ πίνητε ἐπὶ τῆσ τραπέζησ μου ἐν τῇ βασιλείᾳ μου.

In view of these considerations, we may sustain the argument that Jesus intended the observance to be repeated, but we have to return to the question, were the commands to repeat original? We may argue that they were original but that in Mark's form of the tradition they had been omitted to avoid calling attention to the fact that the observance was one which would be repeated. This silence for the sake of security (cf. Jeremias, *Die Abendmahlsworte Jesu*, pp. 118–31) may seem plausible, but have we other comparable instances where material has been suppressed for security?

On the other hand, as we shall see in a later lecture, there is reason why the command should be added if it was not there originally. It is required by a pattern which seems to have been imposed early on the material. This being so, I suggest that the Marcan form is original, but that the commands in 1 Corinthians rightly interpret the intention of the Institution.

A second difference between Mark and 1 Corinthians is this. Mark in his parallel to 'This is my body' has 'This is my blood of the covenant.' 1 Corinthians has 'This cup is the new covenant in my blood.' We can argue that the clause in 1 Corinthians has preserved the older form of the saying, which in Mark has been assimilated to the statement over the bread.

Yet there is a difficulty about this suggestion. 1C. x.16 'The cup of blessing as to which we say the blessing is it not a sharing in the blood of Christ?' and x.21 'You cannot drink the cup of the Lord', and xi.27 'Whoever eats the bread or drinks the cup of the Lord unworthily is guilty of the body and blood of the Lord' – such sentences seem to imply the identification 'This cup is my blood'. On the argument above, this is in conflict with the statement 'This is the new covenant in my blood.' To be guilty of the blood is one thing, to be guilty of the covenant would be another.

A resolution of this difficulty might be as follows: the tradition behind 1 Corinthians originally had, like Mark, 'This is my blood.' As we shall see, this statement may well have created a problem. Partaking of blood was strictly forbidden in the Old Testament. It may be that the statement in the 1 Corinthians tradition was changed from something substantially corresponding to that in Mark to the present form in 1 Corinthians to avoid the suggestion that the faithful were being called upon to drink blood.

We have then two explanations of this difference between the two accounts. One explanation argues that 1 Corinthians is right, and the other that Mark is right. We can now take our choice.

The third difference between the two accounts is also in the declaratory words. Mark has only 'This is my body.' 1 Corinthians adds 'which is for you (τὸ ὑπὲρ ὑμῶν)'. Later Mark has 'this is my blood which is shed for many (τὸ ἐκχυννόμενον περὶ πόλλῶν)'. 1 Corinthians has nothing corresponding to 'which is shed for many' in the declaration over the cup. We may remark that the phrase about the bread in 1 Corinthians is parallel to the phrase about the cup in Mark.

The difference is hard to explain. Mark's phrase attached to the declaration over the cup seems more appropriate than the phrase in 1 Corinthians over the bread. Sacrificial blood, as we shall see, is a concentrate of the power to do away with sins. The fact that the position of τὸ ὑπὲρ ὑμῶν in 1 Corinthians is less appropriate may be an argument in its favour. On the other hand we may be told that the fact that neither expression occurs in both accounts is in favour of neither being original. Perhaps a convincing explanation of this difference has not been advanced. In any case the phrases are evidence for the early understanding of the Institution.

Fourthly Mark has nothing answering to the phrase in 1 Corinthians: μετὰ τὸ δειπνῆσαι 'after having had supper'. 1 Corinthians implies that the action over the bread took place during the meal and that over the cup after it. What does Mark imply?

Before we decide on this, there is one detail to settle. In Mk. xiv.23 many manuscripts have τὸ ποτήριον 'the cup', but others have just ποτήριον 'a cup'. Which is right? There was a tendency in Greek stylists to be sparing in the use of the article. Further, Semitic languages tended to use the corresponding forms often where Greek would do without the article. So it may be here. We should read λαβὼν τὸ ποτήριον, which we may interpret 'taking the cup', where the cup is the well-known cup at the end of the meal. If this is right, though Mark's account is less explicit, it would not imply a different practice.

The alternative would be to argue that Mark's silence would imply a later stage in development when the partaking of the cup was not separated by a large part of the meal from the partaking of bread. Then partaking of bread and cup would come together and 1 Corinthians would have preserved a trace of an older stage in the history of the Eucharist and Mark would be secondary. All we can say is that 1 Corinthians is very archaic here but Mark is not necessarily so.

Finally, Mark has 'my blood of the covenant' and 1 Corinthians 'the new covenant in my blood'. Mark's phrase recalls Exodus xxiv.6–8:

Moses took half of the blood and put it in basins, and half of the blood he threw against the altar. Then he took the book of the covenant, and read it in the hearing of the people; and they said, 'All that the Lord has spoken we will do, and we will be obedient.' And Moses took the blood and threw it upon the people, and said, 'Behold the blood of the covenant which the Lord has made with you in accordance with all these words.'

The new covenant of 1 Corinthians recalls Jeremiah xxxi.31–3:

Behold the days come, says the Lord, when I will make a new covenant with the house of Israel and the house of Judah, not like the covenant which I made with their fathers when I took them by the hand to bring them out of the land of Egypt, my covenant which they broke, though I was their husband, says the Lord. But this is the covenant which I will make with the house of Israel after those days, says the Lord: I will put my law within them, and I will write it upon their hearts; and I will be their God, and they shall be my people. And no longer shall each man teach his neighbour and each his brother, saying, 'Know the Lord', for they shall all know me, from the least of them to the greatest, says the Lord; for I will forgive their iniquity, and I will remember their sin no more.

The choice is easy. Exodus explains the phrase 'blood of the covenant'; Jeremiah has nothing about blood at all. This suggests that 1 Corinthians is secondary in using the word 'new' with its reference to Jeremiah.

What are the results of our comparison? First, Mark is clearly right against 1 Corinthians in having no command to repeat and in avoiding the description of the covenant as new. Secondly, 1 Corinthians has retained explicit evidence for an interval in the observance with the words 'after having had supper'. In the other two differences we can argue either way with a slight implication that Mark is right. Beyond this we notice that in the main fabric of the observance the two accounts are in agreement, a point to which we shall have to return.

LECTURE III

❧

The New Testament accounts: (5) Luke xxii

In the first lecture I maintained that for their account of the Last Supper, Matthew and Luke depended solely on Mark. For Matthew this may cause no difficulty, but you may be surprised that I suggest this for Luke.

You will remember that the scribes who copied the New Testament text over the centuries made two kinds of alteration, mistakes and deliberate changes. I shall first propose that we have to deal with a series of deliberate changes which produced various forms of Luke's text.

In the light of this, let us look at L. xxii.15–20 in Form *A*, as it stands in the Revised Version of 1881, with which the Authorised Version substantially agrees:

(15) He said unto them, 'With desire I have desired to eat this passover with you before I suffer: (16) for I say unto you, I will not eat it, until it be fulfilled in the kingdom of God.' (17) And he received a cup, and when he had given thanks, he said, 'Take this, and divide it among yourselves: (18) for I say unto you, I will not drink from henceforth of the fruit of the vine, until the kingdom of God shall come.' (19) And he took bread, and when he had given thanks, he brake it, and gave to them, saying, 'This is my body which is given for you: this do in remembrance of me.' (20) And the cup in like manner after supper, saying, 'This cup is the new covenant in my blood, even that which is poured out for you.'

We notice one detail that distinguishes this account from the others: whereas they mention only one cup, it mentions two. The Vulgate Gospels, A.D. 384, seem to be the earliest extant witness to Form *A* in the Latin tradition.

This feature already caused trouble in antiquity. One remedy was to remove the reference to the first cup by leaving out verses 17–18 (Form *B*), an alteration we find in one Greek manuscript, the Peshitta Syriac version, and in one Coptic manuscript. The result is something very like the account in 1 Corinthians with the order bread, cup. It does nothing to explain how verses 17–18 got there.

Form *C*, which looks like a variation on this, appears in one early Syriac manuscript (*Sc*):

He took bread and gave thanks and gave it to them saying, 'This is my body which is given for you; do this to proclaim me'; and taking the cup he gave thanks and said, 'Take this and divide it among yourselves; for I say to you that

28

from now on I shall not drink of this fruit of the vine until the kingdom of God comes.'

At first this text looks another attempt to reduce the two cups to one, an explanation, however, which fails to tell us why verses 17–18 are substituted for verse 20. Form B, where verses 17–18 are just left out, seems a more satisfactory way of dealing with this difficulty.

Form D suggests that more is involved. It is the same as Form C except that the second half of verse 19 'which is given for you; do this to proclaim me' is left out as well, an omission which is not accounted for by the hypothesis that the changes were made to eliminate one of the two cups. Form D occurs in two early Latin manuscripts (L b e).

Form E increases our suspicions that more than tidying up is involved. It occurs in the fourth-century Graeco-Latin manuscript Codex Bezae (D) and in four early Latin manuscripts (L a ff^2 i l; *cf.* d). Form E gives us verses 17–19a, omitting 19b and 20 just as Form D does. The only difference is that verses 17–18 remain in the same place as they have in the RV.

The suggestion that Form E was devised to serve the same purpose as Form B, elimination of one of the two cups, encounters an additional difficulty. Forms B, C, D, in reducing the number of cups to one, retain the traditional order. Form E has the order, cup, bread, to which there seems to be no certain parallel in antiquity. It has the following difficulties. It is odd that verses 17–18 should be preferred to verse 20, which has the customary phrasing; the omission of verse 19b is unexplained and, as we have just noticed, the unusual order, cup, bread, is followed.

Is there another explanation of the difference? In this connexion we may notice that the New English Bible and the RSV (1959) follow Codex Bezae and its allies at this point in omitting verses 19b–20, so indicating that these versions regarded this shorter text as original. On this view the RV represents a secondary text.

We have then two contrasted forms of the text, each with its problems, Form A and Form E, and the other forms which seem to derive from them. Form B is probably a derivative of Form A. What about Form C and Form D? They look like attempts to rearrange Form E to give the common order, bread, cup. If that is so, they are derivatives of Form E. These variations can be understood if we regard them as attempts to deal with two different problems: the first is constituted by the RV text and is the presence of the two cups; the second is constituted by the text of the RSV and NEB and is the unusual order, cup followed by bread.

Which Form is original? First we recognise that the vast majority of our extant manuscripts have the longer texts. This however does not help us, as we have been well taught by the nineteenth-century New Testament scholars that manuscripts are not to be counted (*codices non sunt numerandi*).

What looks like a recent attempt to return to counting manuscripts can be found in B. Metzger, *A Textual Commentary on the Greek New Testament* (United Bible Societies, 1971). Here we meet language such as 'impressed by the overwhelming preponderance of external evidence supporting the longer form' (p. 176), 'impressed by the overwhelming external attestation' (p. 184), 'the testimony of the overwhelming mass of witnesses' (p. 297). It is hard to see that 'the overwhelming mass of witnesses' means anything else than the vast majority of witnesses.

The next part of the precept of earlier scholars is more debatable: manuscripts are not to be counted but are to be weighed (*codices non sunt numerandi sed ponderandi*). This of course does not mean that we are to get out a pair of scales and ascertain their physical weight, but that we are to determine their character: are they good or bad witnesses?

Here we touch a controversial matter. Some scholars argue that there are manuscripts of better and worse character as witnesses and that the manuscripts which have the shorter text are inferior, but that among the manuscripts having the longer text are some of excellent character as witnesses.

How do we know whether a manuscript has a good or bad character? We do so from the kind of text it has. If it has a good text, it is a good witness. How do we know whether it has a good text? We learn this by examining the text, not by talking of good and bad manuscripts.

Now let us examine the text at L. xxii.19–20. One question we may ask at once: which form of the text, *A* or *E*, best explains the other? If Form *A* were original would a corrector be likely to produce Form *E* from it, to avoid the presence of two cups for example? Form *B* which removes the first cup does this much better.

If Form *A* fails to explain Form *E*, does Form *E* explain Form *A*? On this showing, *A* with its extra clauses removes the apparent difficulty in *E*, the unusual order, cup, bread, and presents the reader with an account of the institution which would correspond to what he would meet elsewhere. The one difficulty in *A* is that it presents us with two cups. As we have seen, the most likely correction of this is Form *B*, not Form *E*. On this score Form *E* is more likely to explain Form *A* than the other way about.

When I began to study this problem seriously I reached the conclusion, after reading a number of articles on the subject, that, if you were to tell me the name of a man's theological college or seminary, I would be able to predict his conclusions. In order to get away from this state of affairs, where a man's theological formation seemed automatically to determine his conclusions, I looked around for another criterion and I found it in language. I had recently been reading Cadbury, *The Style and Literary Method of Luke*, and this gave me some ideas.

First, the word 'is' came to mind. Greek can dispense with its equivalent ἐστί where 'is' is essential in English. For example a word for word rendering of the beginning of Mark runs as follows: 'The beginning of the gospel of Jesus Christ as it is written'. In English this will not do, and we must write: 'The beginning of the gospel of Jesus Christ is as it is written.'

In 1C. xi.25 we have an equivalent in Greek of this clause: 'This cup is the new covenant.' In the corresponding passage in Luke Form *A* we have 'This cup the new covenant' without the word 'is'. Elsewhere, if Luke's source has 'is', he keeps it, and, if it lacks 'is' he adds it. Here, if 1 Corinthians is Luke's source, Luke has done the direct opposite of what he does elsewhere. His source has 'is' and he has left it out. If Luke and 1 Corinthians had a common source, it is still surprising that Luke should have the form without 'is' and 1 Corinthians the form with it. That Luke should have the form without 'is' and 1 Corinthians have 'is' seems improbable on any showing.

Another point of language concerns the possessives μου and ἐμήν. In the Greek of the New Testament the genitives, μου etc., are rare. In Paul the adjectives are used only attributively, but in Mark and Luke they are not used attributively but only predicatively and pronominally. Paul writes 1C. xi.25 ἐν τῷ ἐμῷ αἵματι ('in my blood'), but Mark in v.19 πρὸσ τοὺσ σούσ ('to your own') and Luke in xv.31 πάντα τὰ ἐμὰ σά εστιν ('all that are mine are yours'). On this argument the expression εἰσ τὴν ἐμὴν ἀνάμνησιν ('to proclaim me') at 1C. xi.24, 25 is regular, but the same phrase at L. xxii.19 conflicts with Lucan usage (see G. D. Kilpatrick, 'The Possessive Pronouns in the New Testament', *JTS*, XLII (1941), 184–6). We now have a second linguistic feature in the longer text at L. xxii.19–20 which is not in keeping with the style of the Gospel.

The preposition 'for' in 'given for you' represents the Greek ὑπέρ, and this recurs at ix.50 only, where we may render the phrase 'on your side'. So we may conclude that ὑπέρ is rare in Luke and appears only here in this sense.

ἀνάμνησισ does not recur in Luke–Acts nor does the corresponding verb ἀναμιμνήσκω. The verb that our author uses elsewhere in this sense is κηρύσσω.

'In the same way', Greek ὡσαύτωσ, reappears for certain only at L. xx.31, though some manuscripts read it at xiii.5. It does not occur in Acts. The Lucan word is ὁμοίωσ 'likewise', which comes some twelve times in Luke.

'After having had supper', translates a Greek idiom, the preposition μετά 'after' followed by the article and the aorist infinitive. The article with the infinitive is common in Luke, occurring over seventy times, but there is only one other example of this form of the idiom where it follows μετά 'after'. We have another feature of style which is unusual in Luke.

Let us now look at the grammatical construction of verse 20. First, the beginning is odd: 'And the cup in the same manner after supper, saying'. There is no subject or main verb here. At the other example of ὡσαύτωσ 'in the same manner' at xx.31, both subject and main verb are expressed. Matthew and Mark have ὡσαύτωσ occasionally, but neither has an example of the word without subject or verb expressed.

Secondly, you may think the declaration was clumsily expressed: 'This cup is the new covenant in my blood, even that which is poured out for you.' The Authorised Version is more straightforward: 'This cup is the new testament in my blood which is shed for you.' Here we suppose that the evangelist is speaking of the shedding of the blood of Jesus. If that is what the makers of the Authorised Version meant, they were not translating the Greek. The Greek can only mean that the cup is poured out, not the blood; to this the rendering of the RV is faithful.

Even to get this rendering demands an unusual construe. 'This cup' at the beginning of the sentence agrees with 'which is poured out for you' at the end over all the intervening words. Such an association seems to be unparalleled in Luke.

The language of the verse and a half of the longer text is not that of Luke. There are the features which are in conflict with Lucan style. There are others which occur very rarely in Luke and there is an un-Lucan confusion of language.

We might think that this would settle the matter, but it has not. We are told that the argument from language does not apply because we are dealing with a liturgical text. This argument assumes that a liturgically important text like the Institution Narrative would retain a fixity of language that would resist the tendency of an author to remove stylistic features which clashed with his own style and to introduce features which agreed with it.

This argument might seem plausible if we had no evidence, but we have evidence. We have the four various accounts in the New Testament and later accounts from Justin, Hippolytus, the ancient liturgies and other sources. While they agree substantially to a large extent, stylistically they differ. As we have already seen, the substantial differences between Mark and Matthew are only one or two, but there are several stylistic changes. In the part of Luke corresponding to Mark there are no substantial changes but some three stylistic ones. Even in Justin's brief account we find one or two. The same tendency to make stylistic changes is to be seen in the liturgies. I conclude that the assertion that the Institution Narrative was stylistically fixed contradicts the facts and that there is evidence that our evangelist himself made stylistic changes in the part of the account that he took over from Mark.

From this I infer that the stylistic differences are relevant and that the language of the longer text is against its belonging to the Gospel.

At this point we may consider the origin of the longer text. The simplest hypothesis is that 19*a* and the phrase in verse 20 'which is poured out for you (τὸ ὑπὲρ ὑμῶν ἐκχυννόμενον)' come from Mark, and that 19*b* and the rest of verse 20 come from 1 Corinthians. The more complicated suggestion is that both Luke and 1 Corinthians derive their accounts from an older source. In principle this is not impossible.

Language gives us a pointer. We have noticed that the longer text has several features which are either contrary to Lucan practice or very rare in it. First we noticed that the possessives were used not according to Lucan style, but according to that of Paul. Secondly, the use of ὑπὲρ 'on behalf of', otherwise unknown in Luke, is common in Paul. Thirdly, the clumsiness in the Lucan declaration, 'This cup is the new covenant in my blood, even that which is poured out for you', disappears in 1 Corinthians.

The account in 1 Corinthians seems to be older. The phrase 'which is on your behalf (τὸ ὑπὲρ ὑμῶν)' is more likely to become 'which is given for you (τὸ ὑπὲρ ὑμῶν διδόμενον)' than the other way about. Again the double command to repeat 'Do this to proclaim me', in 1 Corinthians appears to belong to an older stage in the history of the Eucharist than the single command in Luke.

On the other hand there is nothing in the Lucan account which requires it to be independent of 1 Corinthians. The two or three stylistic differences are the kind of changes that arise in the handing down of a text and constitute no ground for assuming a tradition independent of 1 Corinthians.

Language and older features favour the view that the account in 1 Corinthians is behind that in the longer text of Luke. How then did the theory of Luke's independence of 1 Corinthians come into being?

Like the theory of liturgical immutability, it looks like an expedient to avoid the consequences of the linguistic evidence that the original text of verses 19–20 in Luke is the shorter text of verse 19*a* only. Had some scholars not felt the desperate need to turn the force of this evidence at all costs, we might never have heard of such suggestions.

Let us therefore assume the dependence of Luke on 1 Corinthians and note its peculiarity. Nowhere else in Luke–Acts do we find a verbal dependence on Paul comparable to this. Indeed the remarkable thing is the degree of independence of the Pauline Epistles that our evangelist displays elsewhere in his work. If the longer text is secondary, then this exceptional feature disappears.

To sum up, three considerations suggest that verses 19*b*–20 are a later addition: first, the shorter text is the more difficult; secondly, language favours this; thirdly, elsewhere Luke is verbally independent of the Pauline Epistles. I conclude that the shorter text is right.

I may at this point draw attention to M. Rese, 'Zur Problematik von Kurz- und Langtext in Luk. xxii.17ff', *New Testament Studies*, xxii (1973), 15–31. Rese develops his argument independently of the discussion in this lecture, but his article contains a telling demonstration that the longer text is out of harmony with the Lucan context.

If our evangelist depends on Mark, what has he done? He has taken over Mk. xiv.22 in his verse 19, but has not taken over Mark's verses 23–4, which deal with the cup. As we shall see he uses Mark's verse 25 in two other places.

We say that this is the more difficult text. It is not enough to say this. A text may be so difficult that it is impossible. To avoid this conclusion I must show that the shorter text is difficult, but can be reasonably so explained that we can see the purpose of our evangelist.

We notice that he does not take over Mark's verses 23–4 and does not put anything corresponding in their place. This suggests that he found something offensive in these two verses and if he knew of any other account found the same difficulty there.

Earlier, in the last lecture, when I tried to explain the statement in 1 Corinthians, 'This is the new covenant in my blood' in contrast to Mark's 'This is my blood of the covenant', I recalled that the Old Testament repeatedly and forcefully forbade partaking of blood.

This prohibition may account for our evangelist's failure to use Mark's verses over the cup. Is there anything that supports this?

We notice that in A. xv the text of the Apostolic Decree contains a prohibition of blood. This would be in line with the Old Testament rule and with Jewish practice of the first century A.D. Is there any indication that our author in addition to recording this precept himself took it seriously?

There seems to be one piece of evidence. In the story of the prodigal son (L. xv.11–32), when the son returns to his father the father says: 'Bring the fatted calf, kill it and let us eat and make merry'; but the word that I have rendered 'kill' (θύσατε) really means 'sacrifice'. The dictionaries tell us that though it normally means 'sacrifice' in a few places, it means no more than 'kill'. When we look at these places we find that 'sacrifice' is an acceptable translation except in one connexion.

Once the law of Deuteronomy was established in Israel there was only one place where sacrifice might be made, Jerusalem, a restriction that created a difficulty. The Israelites, like many ancient and primitive peoples, depended largely on sacrifice for their flesh food. The restriction of sacrifice to Jerusalem meant for those who lived at a distance that they would rarely be able to partake of meat. So the law provided a modification; cf. *The Bible Translator*, XII (1961), 130–2.

This modification is to be found in Deuteronomy xii.20–4:

When the Lord thy God shall enlarge thy border, as he hath promised thee, and thou shalt say, 'I will eat flesh', because thy soul desireth to eat flesh; thou mayest eat flesh, after all the desire of thy soul. If the place which the Lord thy God shall choose to put his name there be too far from thee, then thou shalt slaughter of thy herd and of thy flock, which the Lord hath given thee, as I have commanded thee, and thou shalt eat within thy gates, after all the desire of thy soul. Even as the gazelle and as the hart is eaten, so thou shalt eat thereof: the unclean and the clean shall eat thereof alike. Only be sure that thou eat not the blood: for the blood is the life; and thou shalt not eat the life with the flesh. Thou shalt not eat it; thou shalt pour it out upon the earth as water.

The Hebrew word that I have translated 'slaughter' is a sacrificial term זבח and in the LXX is translated by the Greek word for sacrifice, θύσεισ. From this we see that this Greek word has acquired in the Hellenistic Jewish context a second meaning 'to slaughter and drain off the blood', 'to kill kosher', as though it was a reduced kind of sacrifice.

What other examples of this do we find in the New Testament? First in Mt. xxii.4 in his message to his guests the king says 'My fatted beasts have been killed kosher (τεθυμένα)'. They have been slaughtered in the prescribed way for food. J. x.10 has 'The thief does not come except to steal and to kill kosher and to destroy' (θύσῃ). The evangelist distinguishes between killing for food and wanton destruction.

In Luke–Acts, in addition to the Apostolic Decree and the fatted calf for the prodigal son, we find one other striking example of this concern to avoid blood in food. In A. x we have the story of Peter's vision on the house-top at Caesarea. A great sheet on which are all kinds of animals, clean and unclean, is let down from heaven, and Peter is told 'Kill kosher and eat (θῦσον καὶ φάγε).' We are told in effect that the distinction between clean and unclean is done away with, but the prohibition against eating flesh with the blood in it remains. This is supported, as we have seen, by the Apostolic Decree in A. xv. It is also supported by the practice of the ancient Church. Right down to the fourth century we have explicit evidence that Christians did not eat flesh with the blood in it. In this connexion we may notice Rv. xvi.6 'and thou gavest them blood to drink'. This is a requital for the slaughter of the saints and prophets.

It is noticeable that Luke–Acts has more, and more important, references to killing kosher and refraining from blood than any other part of the New Testament. This makes it easier to understand our author's failure to re-produce Mark's verses over the cup with their suggestion of drinking blood.

This explanation however deals with only part of our problem; I still have to account for the other peculiar features of Luke's account, and in particular to justify my assertion that Luke depends exclusively on Mark.

Before I examine the other peculiar features in Luke's account we may look at occasional expressions in Luke–Acts which may be relevant: 'to break bread (κλᾶν ἄρτον)' L. xxii.19, xxiv.30, A. ii.46, xx.7, 11, xxvii.35, 1C. x.16; 'the breaking of bread (ἡ κλάσισ τοῦ ἄρτου)' L. xxiv.35 A. ii.42. The expression also occurs in the accounts of the feeding of the multitude (Mk. vi.41 etc.) and of the Last Supper (Mk. xiv.22–5 etc.).

How far do these passages refer to the Last Supper? Though it is generally held that the accounts of the feeding of the multitude have Eucharistic echoes, it is clear that these accounts do not report a cele-bration of the Eucharist. On the other hand, the instances in the accounts of the Institution clearly do, and with them we may take 1C. x.16.

There remain the passages in Luke–Acts mentioned above. With the apparent exception of A. xxvii.35, they all relate to a group activity.

Before we examine the nature of this activity let us look at A. xxvii.35. The verse as a whole runs: 'And when he had said this and had taken bread he gave thanks to God before all and when he had broken it he began to eat.' At the vital point the text is uncertain:

ἤρξατο ἐσθίειν] + ἐπιδιδοὺσ καὶ ἡμῖν 614 1611 2147 2401 2412 Sh* Cs

It is customary here to print the shorter text and indeed, as far as I know, A. C. Clark is alone in printing the longer text. The longer text, however, has a formal consideration in its favour. It involves a repetition, εσθιε INEπιδιδουσκαιημINEυθυμοιδε. This repetition would make it quite easy for the plus of the longer text to be accidentally omitted. If this longer text is right, then all the examples of breaking of bread in the New Testament occur in a group context.

It may be argued that the longer text in A. xxvii.35 is a later develop-ment to bring this passage into line with the other New Testament pas-sages. As they are all group occasions so must this passage become a group occasion too. This is possible, but is it probable? The suggestion ignores the possibility that scribal error may be responsible and begs the question. The question is: have we any certain example in the New Testament of the breaking of bread outside of a group context? and the answer must be no.

Can we go beyond this? Can we, for example, say whether any or all of these instances are Eucharistic? Let me turn the question round and ask: can any of these instances be certainly shown to be non-Eucharistic?

First, let us look at the accounts of the feeding of the multitude. Quite apart from any other reason why they cannot be occasions of the Eucharist, there is the fact that they antedate the Institution, but it is striking how they enlarge on features which have Eucharistic parallels (Mk. vi.41, viii.6, Mt. xiv.19, xv.36, L. ix.16, J. vi.11), where, at first sight at any rate, this would appear to be unnecessary. This emphasis can be best understood if we assume that the accounts, especially those in the Synoptic Gospels, were concerned to underline an anticipation of the Eucharist.

We notice that the feeding of the multitude seems, from the description of the remnants, to have been a substantial meal. We shall see that the other occasions in question also are in the context of a meal.

How does this help us in our inquiry? We may find it helpful to look first at 1C. x.16 in conjunction with 1C. xi.20: 'when you come together it is not possible to eat the Lord's supper (κυριακὸν δεῖπνον)'. Here the Eucharist is celebrated in the context of a meal. We may conclude that the fact that the breaking of bread takes place in the context of a meal is not in itself a reason for refusing to regard it as a Eucharist.

We may have the greatest doubts about L. xxiv.30, 35, but are these justified? Our difficulties are twofold: first, the occasion is unpremeditated, and secondly, the observance does not seem to be followed through to its conclusion. On the other hand it is as much as any, a messianic occasion, a manifestation of Jesus to his disciples.

When we come to the passages in Acts it is easier to make the identification. A. xx.7, 11 can serve as a parallel to the Pauline Lord's supper. As we have seen, xxvii.35 in the longer text could be such an observance for a small group. The only difficulty about ii.42, 46 is that verse 46 seems, on the following interpretation, to imply a daily Eucharist: 'and daily they continued together in the Temple and broke bread in houses and partook of food'. This interpretation takes 'daily (καθ' ἡμέραν)' as applying to the whole of the verse.

Another interpretation seems possible. According to this, καθ' ἡμέραν refers to the first phrase only, and we can translate: 'and they continued together daily in the Temple and they broke bread in houses' etc. This seems on the whole more probable. There seems to be a clear distinction between (*a*) the activity in the Temple and (*b*) the breaking of bread and partaking of food. If this is so, then 'daily' must refer to the activities in the Temple only.

If we may conclude that 'breaking of bread' in Acts refers to the Eucharist, we have the pertinent question: why is this particular expression used apparently exclusively in Acts for the Eucharist? It recurs twice in the Apostolic Fathers (*Didache* xiv.1, Ignatius, *Eph.* xx.2), but εὐχαριστία, from early times, was the dominant term (Kittel, *TWB* III.729). If the shorter text in L. xxii is original, then the expression 'breaking of bread' is a particularly apposite one. The cup has almost disappeared from the narrative and the breaking and partaking of bread is the climax of the rite. Much more than in Mark or 1C. xi it is the breaking of bread. In this way, with the shorter text at L. xxii, the expression becomes much more understandable for the Eucharist.

I have dealt with the problem of the shorter text in Luke. I now have to try to explain verses 15–18, which are in their proper position distinctive of Luke. In developing my explanation I shall first examine the pieces of which verses 15–18 are composed and secondly attempt to produce an interpretation of this passage as a whole.

Mk. xiv.25 runs: 'Verily I tell you that I shall not again drink of the fruit of the vine until that day when I drink it new in the kingdom of God.' We can see this behind Luke's verse 18: 'For I tell you that I shall not from now on drink of the fruit of the vine until the kingdom of God comes.' Parallel to this is verse 16: 'For I tell you that I shall not eat it until when it is fulfilled in the kingdom of God.' Here 'it' is the passover. On this showing, Mark's verse 25 is the source of Luke's verses 16 and 18. We have to account for the duplication and also the new position for this material.

We can account for most of verse 17 similarly. The first half of the verse repeats parts of Mark's text. 'And taking the cup he gave thanks and said' corresponds to Mark 'And taking the cup he gave thanks . . . and he said to them', except that the Greek word for taking is different. The following words, 'take this', echo Mark's 'take' in verse 23. This leaves only the last clause of verse 17 unexplained: 'and divide it among yourselves'.

Other factors may enter into the explanation of verse 17. Mark may provide formal parallels for the phrasing of much of the verse, but we can find one more substantial in the Jewish *kiddush*. I shall discuss this practice further in lecture v (pp. 66–8 with the quotation from G. F. Moore, *Judaism* (Harvard University Press, 1927), II, 36) but here we may note that if verse 17 reflects the *kiddush* it gives the procedure an obviously Jewish character. As an example of such reshaping we have already seen that the evangelist may have been influenced in his treatment of Mark by the Jewish prohibition of the partaking of blood. Verse 17 would be in keeping with this tendency.

Only verse 15 is left: 'And he said to them, "With desire have I desired to eat this Passover with you before I suffer." ' Here 'to eat this Passover with you' recalls Mk. xiv.14: 'where I may eat the Passover with my disciples'. The word for 'desire' (ἐπιθυμῶ) comes three other times in Luke and once in Acts. Mark and John do not use it at all and Matthew only twice. The combination of noun and verb, 'With desire have I desired', has parallels in our author, A. iv.17 *v.l.* 'let us threaten them with a threat (ἀπειλῇ ἀπειλησώμεθα)', v.28 'commanded you with a command (παραγγελίᾳ παρηγγείλαμεν)', xxiii.14 'we have dedicated ourselves with a dedication (ἀναθέματι ἀναθεματίσαμεν)', with which we may compare what is probably the original text at vii.17, 'the promise which he promised (τῆσ ἐπαγγελίασ ἧσ ἐπηγγείλατο)', and L. xxii.29 *v.l.* 'and I covenant with you a covenant (κἀγὼ διατίθεμαι ὑμῖν διαθήκην).'

We may conclude that verses 15–18 should be explained as based on Mark with some phrases from our evangelist.

Let us look at the elements that we may ascribe to him. These are the references to the Passover and to the sharing the cup. We recall that our evangelist has placed the material at the beginning of the story in contrast to Mark, who has the corresponding verse, xiv.25, at the end. We have noticed that the mention of the cup at this point caused difficulty.

Can we explain these features at one blow? There is one possibility which has already been mentioned, the Passover. We have been accustomed to thinking of the Institution as taking place at a Passover, but if we look closely at the accounts in Mark and 1 Corinthians it is surprising how little evidence we find for this. 1 Corinthians says nothing. Mk. xiv.12–17 does make it quite clear that the occasion was a Passover: 'On the first day of unleavened bread when they used to sacrifice the Passover lamb his disciples said to him, "Where would you have us go and make ready for you to eat the Passover?" ' Apart from these six verses there is nothing in Mark to suggest a Passover if we had not been told so.

This remark raises the question which I shall have to answer: is the Last Supper a Passover or not? To this question I shall return subsequently, but at the moment I am concerned only with the positive details of the New Testament accounts.

It is only in Luke that the presentation is positive and explicit. 'With desire have I desired to eat this Passover with you.' There is nothing like this in Matthew and Mark.

Luke, however, goes further. Despite the resourceful pleading of some scholars, there is in Mk. xiv.18–25 nothing which would prompt us to think of a Passover as distinct from any other occasion. In Luke we can discern several features which recall details of the Passover.

Here let me urge you, if you are ever invited by Jewish friends to attend a Passover, to accept readily and gladly. It is a most instructive and illuminating occasion. Many details which may have been obscure or meaningless to us become significant.

Once I was so invited and I recall one instructive detail. First the Passover meal was got ready. Then, when all was prepared, the wife put a hand towel over her left forearm and a bowl in her left hand and a ewer of water in her right. She came to her husband with her left hand holding out the bowl. He held his fingers over the bowl and she poured water over his fingers and he then wiped his fingers on the towel.

Many of us have seen the same action at the Eucharist. Neither the Jewish Passover nor the Christian Eucharist is likely to have influenced the other in this detail. They both go back independently to first-century practice. Only there can the observance be understood.

If we have not this opportunity, we have the Jewish texts for the observance. First there are the Biblical passages, especially Exodus xii–xiii. Next there is Philo's account in his *Quaestiones in Exodum* i. Third is the *Mishnah* tractate, *Pesach*, with its associated material, and finally there is the Haggada, the manual for the occasion.

From them we can construct the order of the observance as it existed in the first century A.D. After the first cup of wine the head of the family washes his hands in the way we have described. The second cup is mixed and set on the table. The youngest competent boy then asks the following question:

Why is this night different from other nights? For on other nights we eat seasoned food once, but this night twice; on other nights we eat leavened or unleavened bread, but this night all is unleavened; on other nights we eat flesh roast, stewed, or cooked, but this night all is roast (*Pesahim* x.4).

In answer to this the father gives an exposition of the Passover (the Haggada proper) based on two elements, the answers to the questions just mentioned and an exposition of Deuteronomy xxvi.5–11. In the Haggada before me comes first the statement of the obligation to instruct the boy and then this passage:

Blessed be God who keepeth His promise to Israel! Blessed be He!
Blessed be the Lord who determined when the bondage should end, performing that which He promised to our father Abraham in the 'Covenant of the

Pieces', as it is said (Gen. xv.13), 'And God said unto Abraham, Know of a surety that thy seed shall be a stranger in a land that is not theirs, and shall be enslaved; aud shall be afflicted four hundred years; and also that nation, whom they shall serve, will I judge; and afterwards shall they come out with great substance.'

The cup of wine is lifted up while the following is said: And it is this (same promise) that hath been maintained to our forefathers and to us, for there has not been only one to rise up against us to destroy us, but in every generation there have arisen against us those who would destroy us, and the Holy One (blessed be He) has delivered us from their hands.

The cup is replaced on the table:
Enquire and learn what Laban, the Syrian, sought to do to Jacob our father.

Next comes the exposition of Deuteronomy xxvi.5–11 followed by the explanation of the three distinctive features of Passover. The *Mishnah* says:

Rabban Gamaliel used to say: Whosoever has not said [the verses concerning] these three things at Passover has not fulfilled his obligation. And these are they: Passover, unleavened bread, and bitter herbs: 'Passover' – because God passed over the houses of our fathers in Egypt; 'unleavened bread' – because our fathers were redeemed from Egypt; 'bitter herbs' – because the Egyptians embittered the lives of our fathers in Egypt. In every generation a man must so regard himself as if he came forth himself out of Egypt, for it is written, *And thou shalt tell thy son in that day saying, It is because of that which the Lord did for me when I came forth out of Egypt.* Therefore are we bound to give thanks, to praise, to glorify, to honour, to exalt, to extol, and to bless him who wrought all these wonders for our fathers and for us. He brought us out from bondage to freedom, from sorrow to gladness, and from mourning to a Festival-day, and from darkness to great light, and from servitude to redemption; so let us say before him the *Hallelujah* (*Pesahim* x.5).

At the end we have another lifting up of the cup. The text in the Haggada runs as follows:

'And they made their lives bitter with hard bondage, in mortar and in bricks, and in all manner of service in the field; all their service wherein they made them serve was with rigour.'

Lift the cup of wine and say:
Therefore we are in duty bound to thank, to praise, to glorify, to exalt, to honour, to bless, to extol, and to give reverence to Him who performed for us, as well as for our forefathers, all these wonders. He has brought us forth from bondage to freedom, from sorrow to joy, from mourning to festival, from darkness to bright light, and from slavery to redemption. Now, therefore, let us sing before Him a new song, Hallelujah!

Here follows the Hallel, either Psalm cxiii or Psalms cxiii–cxiv. Then the cup is drunk.

To all this we can see parallels in L. xxii.15–18. First, these verses correspond to the Haggada; they give a kind of interpretation of the elements of the observance. Secondly, there is the reference to Passover, with an eschatological exposition of it. Thirdly, there is a taking of the cup with thanksgiving, without an immediate participation. Finally there is an eschatological interpretation of the cup.

There is a certain ambiguity in this treatment. On the one hand, there is an explicit identification with the Passover and, on the other, features of the Last Supper are treated in a way corresponding to what happens in the Passover. The ambiguity is not resolved by saying that for our evangelist the meal is a Passover. As we shall see, it lacks many Passover features. One we have already noticed: the reference to unleavened bread and bitter herbs. As we have seen, the mention of them is an essential of the Passover Haggada, but in Luke they are lacking. The result seems to be that our evangelist has made the occasion more like a Passover without consistently making it a Passover.

If this suggestion is right, we have an explanation of L. xxii.15–18. The materials are derived from Mark and our author has transferred and developed them to make some sense of Mark's identification of the meal with a Passover.

This explanation of these verses has a bearing on our other problem, the text of verses 19–20. I have suggested that the shorter text here is original and that Luke has avoided taking over Mk. xiv.23–4, the verses dealing with the cup, because they commanded the drinking of the blood. The Passover was a sacrifice and so the command would be to drink the blood of a sacrifice, an act even more expressly forbidden:

If any man of the house of Israel or of the strangers that sojourn among them eats any blood, I will set my face against that person who eats blood, and will cut him off from among his people. For the life of the flesh is in the blood; and I have given it for you upon the altar to make atonement for your souls; for it is the blood that makes atonement, by reason of the life. Therefore I have said to the people of Israel, No person among you shall eat blood, neither shall any stranger who sojourns among you eat blood (Leviticus xvii.10–12).

We may now summarise the argument of this chapter. The shorter text of L. xxii.19f is original and xxii.15–19a is the product of two aims of the evangelist, (1) to eliminate the references to blood in the account and (2) to make the observance more like a Passover.

LECTURE IV

❧

The nature of the Eucharist: (1) Passover, sacrifice and the holy

The third lecture treated Luke's account of the Last Supper. Part of the argument dealt with the evangelist's attempt to make the Last Supper look more like a Passover. In making this suggestion I obliquely raised the question: 'Is the Last Supper a Passover?' We may now go on to ask: 'If it is not a Passover, what is it?' It is with these questions that we shall now concern ourselves.

At first sight there seems to be no question. As we saw, Mk. xiv.12–17 is explicit: the forthcoming meal is a Passover. Matthew and Luke repeat this information without question. The only difficulty we might find in this is that when we get to the account of the meal in Mark and Matthew it does not read like an account of a Passover.

Our real difficulty comes when we turn to John. Mk. xiv.12 reads 'And on the first day of unleavened bread when they used to sacrifice the Passover lamb his disciples said to him: "Where would you have us go and make ready for you to eat the Passover?" ' This is followed by Matthew and Luke and is clear enough. The Passover lambs were slaughtered that afternoon and the Passover meal took place that night. Jesus' arrest and appearance before the Sanhedrin followed. The next morning he was brought before Pilate, who condemned him to death, crucifixion followed and Jesus died about 3 o'clock that afternoon.

John agrees in the main in the sequence of events as far as they concern Jesus but not about the placing of the Passover in relation to these events. Jesus has the evening meal with his disciples. Afterwards he is arrested and brought before Annas and Caiaphas and the following morning before Pilate. Here we have our first disagreement, J. xviii.28 'They did not themselves enter the praetorium in order not to be defiled but to eat the Passover.' This is quite clear, that the Passover has not yet taken place on the morning before Jesus' crucifixion.

Later at the crucifixion we have J. xix.14 'It was the preparation for the Passover; it was about the sixth hour.' This is supported by J. xix.31 'Since it was the preparation, in order that the bodies should not remain on the cross on the sabbath, for that day of the sabbath was a great day, they asked Pilate that their legs should be broken and that they should be removed.' In other words Passover and sabbath fell together. This being so, Jesus died upon the cross at about the time when the Passover lambs were slaughtered, though John does not say so explicitly.

With this agrees J. xiii.1–2 'Before the Passover feast, Jesus knowing that his hour had come to depart from this world, loved them to the end. And during supper . . . ' This makes it clear that for John the Last Supper was not a Passover. The events in Jesus' life, supper, arrest, trial, crucifixion remain the same, but the Passover is a day later. With this agrees J. xiii.29 'Some thought, since Judas had the purse, that Jesus said to him "Buy what we have need of for the feast." ' It is improbable that Judas would get up from the Passover meal to buy what was needed for it, or that he would find a Jew to sell to him. This again supports the general tenor of John's account.

This avoids one great difficulty presented by Mk. xiv.12–16: the Passion takes place during the festival. It would have been impossible for conservative Sadducee and radical Pharisee alike to take part in these events during Passover. On John's account there is no difficulty; the Passion is over before the Passover begins.

John's placing of the Passover has one piece of supporting evidence from 1C. v.7 'For Christ our Passover has been sacrificed for us.' This remark would have more point if the death of Christ and the slaughter of the Passover lambs took place at the same time. It is not itself conclusive in favour of the position of the Passover as is the account in John, but as far as it goes it supports John. On the other hand there is no reference to the Passover in the account of the Last Supper in 1 Corinthians. Indeed the verse we have just quoted is the one reference to the Passover in the Pauline Epistles.

As we have noticed, the evidence of John is in agreement with the implications of Mk. xiv.17–25. Here the distinctive features of Passover are all lacking and Mark's report in these verses could be quite easily associated with the Johannine placing of the Passover on the next evening.

Many attempts have been made to reconcile Mk. xiv.12–16 with John's account, but with all their resource and subtlety they do not prove convincing. The best known of these is by Professor J. Jeremias of Göttingen and though I remain unconvinced I readily admit a great debt to him for his most instructive book on the subject, *The Eucharistic Words of Jesus* as it is called in its English form. Far and away the best discussion known to me of the various suggestions is by Dr George Ogg, *The Chronology of the Last Supper*, in *Historicity and Chronology in the New Testament*, S.P.C.K. Theological Collections VI (1965), pp. 75–96. I shall not take you through these suggestions myself, but refer you to his well-informed and judicious examination.

One statement connected with the tradition that the Last Supper was a Passover will prove important, Mk. xiv.12 'The first day of unleavened bread when they were sacrificing the Passover'. This makes it quite clear that for those sources which had this tradition, the Last Supper was a sacrifice or at least sacrificial.

Is there any support for this view apart from the Passover tradition? The principal account which is independent of it is that in 1 Corinthians. We may examine the features common to 1 Corinthians and Mark to see if they support the view that the Last Supper was a sacrifice.

First we notice again the clause at 1C. xi.24, 'this is my body which is for you', and in Mk. xiv.24 'this is my blood of the covenant which is shed for many'. We may think that here we have a reference to Christ's death on the cross as sacrificial which associates the Eucharist with that death and sacrifice. I shall return later to this association, but at present I am concerned with the question: are these expressions 'for you', 'shed for many' sacrificial?

In the first lecture I suggested to you that vicarious death and vicarious suffering were not necessarily sacrificial. They could be so, but not because they were vicarious, done or suffered on behalf of others. You may well ask me: 'If death or suffering on behalf of others is not a sacrifice, what, pray, is a sacrifice?'

This question forces us to face the question which I have hitherto avoided: 'What is a sacrifice?' You will remember that the first lecture hinted at this question, but there I limited myself to the warning that sacrifice in the Ancient World was something quite different from what our use of the word implies. Their institution was not the same as our picture of it.

I shall draw our information about sacrifice mainly from the Bible, the practice of the ancient Greeks and Romans, and the evidence of the Ancient Middle East. We can find comparable institutions elsewhere, particularly among ancient and primitive peoples.

It has been one of the handicaps of Christian theology that it lost contact at a certain period with this background. The result in Western Christendom was an *a priori* reconstruction of what sacrifice was which determined the teaching of the Scholastic theologians of the Middle Ages and the debates of the sixteenth century. This development is admirably indicated in F. C. N. Hicks, *The Fullness of Sacrifice* (Macmillan, 1930), especially in Part III. From this book we see clearly how the Biblical view of sacrifice is sustained until the fourth and fifth centuries A.D., when the contact with the institution as a living practice was lost. Only then did the hypothetical reconstruction become possible which we can discern in the medieval theologians.

Let us turn then to the Bible, where sacrifice is so important an institution, and consider the various kinds of sacrifice we find there. When I was reading theology at Oxford I was taught that there were three basic types: communion sacrifice, gift sacrifice and atonement sacrifice. The worshippers took part in communion sacrifices but not in the other two kinds. The question to which various answers were given was: 'which of the three was basic to the other two?'

W. O. E. Oesterley in his book, *Sacrifices in Ancient Israel* (H. & S., 1937), pp. 33–41, suggested an additional type of sacrifice, sacrifice as releasing and conferring life and power. This type he placed alongside the others as explaining more adequately than they a whole series of sacrifices.

I shall use Oesterley's suggestion but develop it to provide the explanation of the three main kinds of sacrifice mentioned just now. In this way the gift sacrifice is one in which life and power are given to the god. Similar to this are consecratory sacrifices, in which power is conveyed, for example, to an altar or a priest. In the communion sacrifice, life and power are conveyed to god and worshipper alike. In expiatory sacrifice, life and power are released to do away with offences, the implication being that they could not otherwise be eliminated. It is noteworthy that on this theory a reference to a god is not an essential feature of sacrifice and we can recall instances in the historic religion of Israel where the reference to God is not obvious.

In this connexion we may notice the importance of blood. We are told that it is the life, as we have seen in the passage Deuteronomy xii.20–5 quoted in lecture III (cf. Leviticus xvii.11, 14). We notice in Exodus the use of blood at the Passover (Exodus xii), at the Covenant at Sinai (Exodus xxiv.5–8) and at the consecration of Aaron and his sons (Exodus xxix). Leviticus, Numbers and Deuteronomy have many references to blood in sacrifice.

With this importance of blood may be associated its reservation for God alone. This was not always so. In Passover it was sprinkled on the lintels of the doors, in the account of the Covenant at Sinai it is sprinkled on the people, and in the consecration of Aaron and his sons blood is put on the right ear, the right thumb, the right great toe of each of them. The throwing of blood on the altar may not be an example of this because there is some reason for thinking that in early times the altar was identified with God.

Later tradition modified the account of the Covenant at Sinai in one particular. From the early centuries A.D. we have a number of Aramaic renderings or Targums of the Old Testament. As Professor A. Diez Macho of Madrid has pointed out in *MS Neophyti I*, vol. II: 'Exodo' (Consejo Superior de Investigaciones Científicas, 1970), p. 156 n.8 two of these renderings have a significant variation at Exodus xxiv.8 'And Moses took the blood and tossed it upon the people.' For this the Targums of Onkelos and Ps.-Jonathan have: 'And Moses took the blood and tossed it upon the altar to propitiate for the people.' In this way, though the people benefit from the blood, they cease to receive it; they no longer partake in it. This may be a parallel to L. xxii.19 as I explained it; the evangelist has avoided a command to partake of the blood. This of course does not affect the institution of sacrifice in principle.

To sacrifice let us return, and to some examples of it. In 2 Kings iii is the story of the attempt of Israel with the help of Judah and Edom to sub-due Mesha, king of Moab, who had rebelled against Israel. The allies had overrun the country and were about to assault the city when the king of Moab 'took his eldest son who was to reign in his place and offered him for a burnt offering upon the wall. And there was great wrath upon Israel and they departed from him and returned to their own land' (2 Kings iii.27).

Several points are of interest in this story, but one question is important: why did the king sacrifice his son upon the wall? We may suppose that there were altars and places of sacrifices enough in the city where the boy could be sacrificed. Why then upon the wall? If a sacrifice was a release of life and power as this one could be thought to be, then we may conclude that the life and power were released to strengthen the wall to throw back the enemy, as seems to have happened; 'there was great wrath upon Israel'. The New English Bible mistranslates: 'The Israelites were filled with such consternation at this sight.'

Another example of sacrifice serving to strengthen a material object, a thing as distinct from gods or men, may be found in the account of the Passover in Egypt (Exodus xii). The Israelites were to dip a bunch of hyssop into the blood of the Passover lamb and apply the blood to the lintel and the doorposts of the house, and no Israelite was to go out before morning. 'For the Lord will pass through to slay the Egyptians and when he sees the blood upon the lintel and on the two doorposts the Lord will pass over the door and will not allow the destroyer to come into your houses to slay you' (Exodus xii.23). As the story now stands, the blood on the lintel and doorposts is a kind of notice, 'Keep out', but we may suspect that to begin with the destroyer did his rounds alone and the blood was intended to reinforce the doorway to prevent him from coming in and killing.

An example of sacrifice reinforcing action is to be found in the story of Balaam and Balak, king of Moab, in Numbers xxii–xxiv. Balak sent for Balaam to curse Israel and Balaam came and

. . . said to Balak, 'Build for me here seven altars, and provide for me here seven bulls and seven rams.' Balak did as Balaam had said; and Balak and Balaam offered on each altar a bull and a ram. And Balaam said to Balak, 'Stand beside your burnt offering, and I will go; perhaps the Lord will come to meet me; and whatever he shows me I will tell you.' And he went to a bare height. And God met Balaam; and Balaam said to him, 'I have prepared the seven altars, and I have offered upon each altar a bull and a ram.' And the Lord put a word in Balaam's mouth, and said, 'Return to Balak, and thus you shall speak.' And he returned to him, and lo, he and all the princes of Moab were standing beside his burnt offering. And Balaam took up his discourse, and said,

> 'From Aram Balak has brought me,
>   the king of Moab from the eastern mountains:
> "Come, curse Jacob for me,
>   and come, denounce Israel!" ' (Numbers xxiii.1–7)

The action is repeated twice. Each time, while the bullock and the ram are burning on the altar, Balaam takes up his stand to curse Israel and each time God commands him to bless. What part do the sacrifices play in all this? We may infer that they are offered to reinforce the curse or the blessing with the life and strength so released. We notice that the power conferred by sacrifice may be used for good or ill, for curse or blessing.

From Homer onward the Greeks had an expression for making a covenant, ὅρκια τέμνειν 'to cut oath sacrifices', where 'cut' does not mean 'divide in two' but just 'sacrifice' in general. The Greek word ὅρκοσ, which we translate 'oath', meant the object on which an oath was taken. A man could swear by Styx, for example, and it may be that the sacrifices were intended to empower Styx to destroy him if he did not keep his oath.

The Old Testament had a similar expression קרת כרית 'to cut a covenant', though what a *berîth* was to begin with is still unknown. It is usually assumed that 'cut' meant to divide, and this would fit in with the account of the covenant in Genesis xv.9–10:

He said to him 'Bring me a heifer three years old, a she-goat three years old, a ram three years old, a turtledove, and a young pigeon.' And he brought him all these, cut them in two, and laid each half over against the other; but he did not cut the birds in two.

Unfortunately the word here for 'cut in two' is not קרת but בתר 'divide' and so we cannot argue that 'cut' in the phrase 'cut a covenant' means 'divide'.

The Old Testament knew at least two kinds of covenant sacrifice. One is that already alluded to in the previous paragraph, in the same chapter of Genesis, verse 17 'When the sun went down and it was dark, behold a smoking furnace and a flaming torch that passed between these pieces.' With this we may compare Jeremiah xxxiv.18: 'And I will give the men that have transgressed my covenant, who have not established my covenant which they cut before me, the calf which they divided and passed between the parts of it . . .' In these accounts the victim or victims are divided in two and the maker of the covenant passes between the parts.

As we can recall, the occasion is different at Sinai in Exodus xxiv.5–8:

And he sent young men of the children of Israel, which offered burnt offerings, and sacrificed peace offerings of oxen unto the Lord. And Moses took half of the blood, and put it in basons; and half of the blood he sprinkled on the altar. And he took the book of the covenant, and read in the audience of the people: and they said, 'All that the Lord hath spoken will we do, and be obedient.' And Moses took the blood, and sprinkled it on the people, and said, 'Behold the blood of the covenant, which the Lord hath made with you concerning all these words.'

Here the blood is the effective element in the sacrifice and is tossed on altar and people, presumably the two contracting parties.

We hear of other examples of covenant sacrifice. For example in one part of the Ancient Middle East men sacrificed an ass, a victim forbidden in Israel. The making of covenant by sacrifice also existed in the Roman world as we know by the Latin expressions *icere, ferire pactum* 'to strike an agreement', where *icere, ferire* indicate the sacrificial action. Throughout the ancient world the covenant was made with sacrifice and some covenants with sacrificial blood.

Though, in this story of Balaam, sacrifice can reinforce a curse as well as a blessing, bring disaster as well as prosperity, in the examples I have discussed sacrifice strengthens the consequences willed by the sacrificer. We can now look at an example where sacrifice is potent and brings disaster, but does not fulfil the will of the sacrificer.

In Numbers xvi Korah and his company challenge the pre-eminence of Moses and Aaron on the grounds that not they alone but all the congregation is holy. Moses in reply issues a challenge: (Numbers xvi.5–7)

In the morning the Lord will shew who are his, and who is holy, and will cause him to come near unto him. This do; take you censers, Korah, and all his company; and put fire therein, and put incense upon them before the Lord tomorrow: and it shall be that the man whom the Lord doth choose, he shall be holy: ye take too much upon you, ye sons of Levi.

Korah and his company offered incense in this way and perished: 'And fire came forth from the Lord, and devoured the two hundred and fifty men that offered the incense' (Numbers xvi.35). The Lord commanded Eleazer 'to take up the censers out of the burning and scatter the fire far and wide, for they are holy' (Numbers xvi.36). Burning incense was itself an offering. Like any sacrifice it could be mishandled, and then the power released could break loose and destroy. We notice in this connexion the appearance of the word 'holy'.

In 2 Chronicles xxvi King Uzziah offended in a way similar to that of Korah 'and entered the temple of the Lord to burn incense on the altar of incense' (xxvi.16). He was stricken with leprosy for his offence.

From this it is clear that the power released in sacrifice could take a wrong turning and bring disaster. Precautions had to be taken against this, and we find rules for such precautions in the laws of the Pentateuch. Sacrifice, for example, might only take place in the authorised area at the appointed place. It had to proceed according to prescribed form and with duly authorised ministers. Those present had to be properly clothed and in a fit state. In fact the world was divided into two, the place and conditions in which superhuman power could be safely released in sacrifice, and the rest of the world and the conditions in which it could not. The former was holy and the latter profane.

Let me illustrate this. 1 Samuel vi.19f gives an example of the danger of profane behaviour with the holy:

And he slew some of the men of Bethshemesh, because they looked into the ark of the Lord; and he slew seventy of them, and the people mourned because the Lord had made a great slaughter among the people. Then the men of Bethshemesh said, 'Who is able to stand before the Lord, this holy God?'

Another example occurs at 1 Samuel xxi.1–6. David asked for provisions for himself and his companions from Abimelech, the priest of Nob.

And the priest answered David, 'I have no common bread at hand, but there is holy bread; if only the young men have kept themselves from women.' And David answered the priest, 'Of a truth women have been kept from us as always when I go on an expedition; the vessels of the young men are holy, even when it is a common journey; how much more today will their vessels be holy?' (1 Samuel xxi.4–5).

War was an operation when extraordinary power was in demand and so the Hebrew expression for 'to make war' was 'to consecrate war'. The ancient Romans had similar expressions and interesting customs and prohibitions connected with this condition of war.

The words for 'holy' in various languages are instructive. The Germanic languages have a group of words which are ambivalent. The ambivalence can be seen most clearly in German. If we take the word *Heil* it means 'salvation' as in *Heilsarmee* 'Salvation Army' and also 'health, vigour, strength', so that we can understand the greeting *Heil* and the wish *Sieg*

Heil. Heil is the noun and the adjective is *heilig*, but they do not correspond in meaning. The same development has taken place in its English equivalent, 'holy', but in English we have another form of the adjective, namely 'hale' in which the meaning 'strong, vigorous' has survived. Thus the two languages have associated this group of words with two meanings: (1) *heilig* and 'holy', what we may call the religious sense, and (2) *Heil*, 'health, welfare', 'wholesome, hale', and the like, where the sense of strength, vigour, well-being is manifest.

How are these two meanings associated with words that derive from the same root? The nouns *Heil* and 'health' may give us the clue with their meaning 'vigour, strength and power'. In a religious context this may mean a great power outgoing for good or ill. Because of this power the person or thing in which it resides may be called *heilig*, 'holy'.

Greek has a similar ambivalence. One of the words for 'holy' is ἱερόσ. Words in English like 'hierarchy' are derived from it and we meet it occasionally in the Greek Bible. But in older Greek it has another meaning. The sixth-century poet, Alcman, wrote a poem for a choir of girls in which he probably described them as ἱερόφωνοι. By this he did not mean that the girls had holy voices. He meant that they had good strong voices. In the same way the Greek poets use the adjective ἱερόσ in a number of phrases where it seems to mean 'violent, strong', for example ἱερὸν κῦμα 'a mighty wave' (Euripides, *Hippolytus* 1206f). Again we have the two meanings 'strong' and 'holy'. Sometimes we cannot be sure what is intended. In Homer we have the expression Ἴλιοσ ἱρή. We translate it 'holy' or 'sacred Troy', but it may mean 'strong Troy'. Another expression is Τροίησ ἱερὰ κρήδεμνα, surely 'the strong battlements of Troy' (*Iliad* xvi.100).

We seem to have another ambivalence, only this time the two meanings are contained in the same word. 'Strong, mighty' would be the original meaning and 'holy' would be the derivative. We can imagine a connexion in the instance of Troy. Troy is strong with superhuman strength because the gods are there.

When we turn to Latin and Hebrew we do not find such ambivalences. We do not know the basic meaning of the Latin words for 'holy' *sacer* and *sanctus*. The traditional interpretation of *sacer* is that it describes something or someone that has been made over to the gods, but this does not explain certain features, connected with the word. For example, in the Twelve Tables the criminal is condemned – *sacer esto* ('let him be holy') – but he can be treated in a way that suggests that he has dangerous power. Hence we may infer that whatever the etymology of *sacer* it describes something or someone as having superhuman power that can work for good or ill.

At this point we may notice an interesting equation. To express the meaning 'sacrifice' the Greeks had a number of phrases: ἱερὰ ἔρδειν, ἱερὰ ποιεῖν, ἱερὰ ῥέζειν. Latin had one corresponding term *sacrificare*. Granted that we do not know the original meaning of *sacer*, we can none the less construct this parallel

$$\left. \begin{array}{l} \text{ἱερὰ ποιεῖν} \\ \text{ἔρδειν} \\ \text{ῥέζειν} \end{array} \right\} sacri\text{-}ficare$$

and note the basic similarity of the expressions, where ἱερά corresponds to *sacer* or *sacra* and ποιεῖν etc. corresponds to *-ficare*. As evidence for an earlier variety in Latin we may cite *sacerdos*. Basically the meaning seems to be the same in both languages, 'to convert into things of power' and to describe the release of life and power which is associated with ἱερόσ and assists its semantic migration from 'strong' to 'holy'. We may notice that this line of interpretation conflicts with a view that goes back to antiquity, according to which ἱερόσ has a theological reference. We have noticed that in sacrifice in the Old Testament the theological reference is some-times lacking and we may suspect that the same is true for sacrifice among other ancient peoples. If this is true, we may infer that in Greek and Roman religion as in that of the Old Testament the theological was steadily extended until it was impossible to think of sacrifice without it. I shall return shortly to this point.

The Hebrew root קדש seems to mean 'to be set apart' originally and so 'to be hallowed, consecrated'. It describes a symptom of the condition. Whatever is possessed of superhuman power has to be set apart for safety's sake. As we have seen the regulations of the Pentateuch, especially from Exodus onward, frequently have as their aim the separating of the holy from the profane and we have noticed instances of disaster where this separation broke down.

My interpretation of the idea of the holy conflicts with a common view since the work of the German theologian R. Otto. In his book, *The Idea of the Holy* (Oxford University Press, 1936), this is equated with the numinous. Where God is felt as present, there we are before the holy. God is holy and all holiness is derived from his presence and we associate the word 'holy' with the awareness of his presence.

There is an element of truth in this. God as a pre-eminent source of superhuman life and power is holy, but he is not alone in this. A censer, even after misadventure, is holy, as we have seen, and in ancient Roman law a criminal can be *sacer* or holy too. We notice that the strength of God or the gods is emphasised in the Old Testament. One of the words for God, אל, is said to have this meaning. In Psalm lxxviii.25 'Man did eat the bread of the mighty (לחם אבירים)', 'the bread of the mighty' is the food of the gods, an idea to which I shall return in the next lecture, but meanwhile we notice this unusual term for 'mighty' as a designation of the gods.

This exploration of the institution of sacrifice and the idea of the holy began as an answer to the question: what is a sacrifice? and I encountered this question when I attempted to answer a prior one: is the Eucharist a sacrifice? It is now time to return to this first question.

We noticed that for those who held, like the Synoptic Gospels, that the Last Supper was a Passover, it followed that the Last Supper was a sacrifice, but that for those who did not hold this view, this argument did not apply.

This is particularly true of 1 Corinthians. There is no evidence that for Paul the Last Supper was a Passover. Is there any other evidence that he regarded it as a sacrifice? Two pieces of evidence may be brought forward. Both are in 1C. xi.27–30:

Wherefore whosoever shall eat the bread or drink the cup of the Lord unworthily, shall be guilty of the body and the blood of the Lord. But let a man examine himself, and so let him eat of the bread, and drink of the cup. For he that eateth and drinketh, eateth and drinketh judgement unto himself if he separate not the body. For this cause many among you are weak and sickly, and and not a few are at rest.

First, we notice the odd remark in the last verse. When I have been instructing candidates for confirmation, for example, I have told them that unworthy reception at the Eucharist leads to hardening of conscience and difficulty of repentance, but not that many of them would be ill and some would die. Nor do I suspect have you so taught or been taught. Why then did the Apostle write this sentence which many commentators have been glad to pass over quickly?

The answer can be found in two stories we looked at earlier, the story of Korah and his company and the story of King Uzziah. As we say, Korah and those with him presumed on a sacrifice; they offered incense out of turn and were destroyed. King Uzziah did the same was stricken with leprosy. Here we have our two parallels, Uzziah for those who are sick and ill, and Korah and his fellows for those who died for unworthy receiving. In each case the virtue of the sacrifice which should have been for the good of the participants turns to their ruin when they come unworthily to it.

The second piece of evidence in this passage lies in the phrase μὴ διακρίνων τὸ σῶμα 'not separating the body'. Elsewhere in this passage σῶμα is the body of the Lord, the Eucharistic bread, and we may assume that this is its meaning here. It is hard to see what the traditional rendering 'not discerning the body' means. διακρίνειν means 'to separate, distinguish'. 'Not separating the body' will mean treating it as something profane and, as we saw, the distinction between profane and holy was important in sacrifice. Here the offenders ignore it to their detriment. Photius has rightly interpreted the phrase: μὴ διακρίνων τὸ σῶμα τοῦ κυρίου, ἀλλ' ὡσ ἀδιαφόρῳ τῶν λοιπῶν μετέχων αὐτοῦ καὶ προσερχόμενοσ αὐτῷ 'not distinguishing the body of the Lord but partaking of it and approaching it like something undistinguished from the rest') (K. Staab, *Pauluskommentare aus der griechischen Kirche* (Aschendorff, 1933), p. 569).

If my exegesis is right, these two expressions in 1C. xi.27–30 show that Paul himself understood the Eucharist as a sacrifice. This conclusion does not automatically carry with it the demonstration that Jesus so regarded it. Can we produce evidence that from its institution the Eucharist was so intended?

There is one piece of such evidence. Common to both Mark and 1 Corinthians is the association of covenant and blood in the utterance over the cup. We noticed earlier the two forms of this saying; Mk. xiv.24, 'This is my blood of the covenant', and 1C. xi.25, 'This cup is the new covenant in my blood', and I discussed their differences. Now we look at what they have in common, the reference to blood and covenant. As we have seen, covenants in the ancient world were made with sacrifice, but at Sinai we have the details of a particular kind of covenant sacrifice which was made with blood. To this the saying at the Last Supper refers, a reason, you will recall, for thinking that the adjective 'new' in 1 Corinthians is out of place as introducing a reference away from Sinai to Jeremiah's new covenant (Jeremiah xxxi.31–4). Jesus in effect is saying that the Last Supper is his covenant sacrifice with his own, just as Sinai was Yahweh's covenant sacrifice with his people.

Granted that the Last Supper was a sacrifice with power, what did it achieve? To this question we can perhaps detect two answers in the New Testament. The first comes in Mt. xxvi.28 and the second in J. vi.48–71. We shall notice a supplementary consideration.

We have remarked one substantial difference at Mt. xxvi.28 from Mk. xiv.24. Mark ends with 'poured out for many', but Matthew adds 'for the remission of sins'. If we can think of first-century Christians asking what good the Eucharist achieved as a sacrifice, we can regard this phrase as an answer well in line with the Old Testament.

In the Old Testament there were many expiatory sacrifices, and in these blood played a most important part, as at the Day of Atonement (Leviticus xvi):

Aaron shall present the bullock of the sin offering, which is for himself, and shall make atonement for himself, and for his house, and shall kill the bullock of the sin offering which is for himself (verse 11).

. . . and he shall take of the blood of the bullock, and sprinkle it with his finger upon the mercy-seat on the east; and before the mercy-seat shall he sprinkle of the blood with his finger seven times. Then shall he kill the goat of the sin offering, that is for the people, and bring his blood within the veil, and do with his blood as he did with the blood of the bullock, and sprinkle it upon the mercy-seat and before the mercy-seat (verses 14–15).

We can see the addition in Matthew in the light of such Old Testament antecedents.

The second possible answer in J. vi. has a different background, but before we look at this let us consider the structure of the chapter. The section vi.1–15 is the account of the feeding of the multitude. The section vi.26–51 reads like an exposition of this feeding except for the clause at verse 35 'He who believes on me shall in no wise ever thirst', a statement which takes up iv.14 'Whoever drinks of the water which I shall give him shall in no wise thirst for ever.' Otherwise all is in terms of bread and eating.

Verse 51, 'I am the living bread which came down from heaven. If anyone eats of this bread he will live for ever; and the bread which I shall give is my flesh on behalf of the life of the world', is a kind of watershed. It looks back to the previous exposition and points forward to a fresh development. For the first time in the exposition the bread is called 'my flesh'.

Almost at once the parallel appears in verse 54 'He who eats my flesh and drinks my blood has eternal life and I shall raise him up at the last day.' The Gospel has now left the feeding of the multitude behind. We can relate Jesus' flesh to the bread of the feeding, but there is nothing in that event as told corresponding to his blood. The Gospel is now expounding the Eucharist, in particular the flesh and blood of the Lord as bestowing eternal life. Here we have our second answer to our question. The Eucharist gives eternal life.

There is a background to this theme quite as ancient as the theme of expiation that we were discussing in connexion with Matthew. In Homer the gods differ from men in degree. They are men writ large except for one thing. Men are mortal and they are immortal. Connected with this is, as we might expect, the fact that they have different food. They drink nectar and eat ambrosia. And what does ambrosia mean? It means immortality. Homer does not say in so many words that the gods are immortal because they eat immortality, but others said it for him and it is implied by what he says.

This idea that there is a food of immortality appears also in other parts of the ancient world and in the Old Testament. Genesis iii tells of the two trees in Eden, the tree of the knowledge of good and evil, and the tree of life. Man ate of the tree of the knowledge of good and evil and

Then the Lord God said, 'Behold, man has become like one of us, knowing good and evil, and now, lest he put forth his hand and take also of the tree of life and eat and live for ever' . . . he drove out the man; and at the east of the garden of Eden he placed the cherubim, and a flaming sword which turned every way, to guard the way to the tree of life (Genesis iii.22, 24).

Here we have an example of the food of immortality. The expression 'tree of life' recurs several times in Revelation (ii.7, xxii.2, 14, 19).

Another instance in the Old Testament is the manna in the wilderness. The account in Exodus xvi does not help us but we have already quoted Psalm lxxviii.25 'Man ate of the bread of the mighty ones.' Manna is the food of the gods, and we may infer that it gave them immortality. The Psalm verse is echoed in Wisdom xvi.20 'Instead of these things thou didst give thy people the food of angels, and without their toil thou didst supply them from heaven with bread ready to eat, providing every pleasure and suited to every taste.' This manna seems to have given rise to the expression 'bread of life', which appears in the Hellenistic romance *Joseph and Asenath* before it recurs in John.

This theme of the bread of life explains 1C. x.1–11. In the wilderness on their way from Egypt to Palestine, the Israelites had eaten manna and drunk water from the rock, the spiritual food and the spiritual drink, and yet they died. Surprisingly at first sight this constitutes a problem for the Apostle and he implies that he expected them not to die. 'Nevertheless with most of them God was not pleased; for they were overthrown in the wilderness.' We can see the difficulty. Having taken spiritual food and drink they should live for ever, but they failed to do so. Why was this? They displeased God with their evil conduct and so despite the spiritual food they died. If this interpretation is right, the Apostle has understood the manna and the water as being the food and drink of immortality.

This thesis that the Eucharist is the food of immortality was taken up in the Christian interpretation and liturgy. Within a generation of John, Ignatius says: 'breaking one loaf which is the medicine of immortality' (*Eph*. xx.2). The words in the Tridentine Missal for the celebrant were: 'Corpus domini nostri Jesu Christi custodiat animam meam in uitam aeternam.' In some places the English liturgy still says: 'The body of our Lord Jesus Christ preserve thy body and soul unto everlasting life.'

As we would expect in any sacrifice, the Eucharist releases superhuman life and strength, the life and strength of the Lord. So it avails to do away with sin and to convey eternal life. I do not suggest that Christians of the first century thought of the Eucharist as achieving only these two things. Indeed there is evidence to the contrary.

This evidence is negative. We are used to the definition of the Eucharist as consisting of an outward and visible sign and an inward and spiritual grace, as the description of a sacrament. As we saw in the first lecture, this notion is as old as Augustine but no older. The Bible does not know it.

We may be tempted to think that this absence of the word 'sacrament' from the Bible is a mere matter of words and that the fact of sacrament is there even if the word is missing. In a sense this is true and we can acknowledge this truth by saying that the religion of the Bible is sacramental, but the silence of the Bible goes further.

The definition of sacrament that I have just quoted refers to 'an inward and spiritual grace'. 'Grace' as a theological reality is already a well-developed notion in the New Testament, but we do not find it associated with the Eucharist there. It is curious for example that in Paul's several references to the Eucharist he does not mention grace at all.

In acknowledging this, we do not say that the later definition of the Eucharist is mistaken nor do we suggest that it is merely a memorial meal with no more than a sentimental appeal. If we started only from the failure of the New Testament to associate Eucharist and grace, this would be a natural conclusion especially if we understand ἀνάμνησισ as 'memory' or 'memorial'.

Early Christian liturgical practice, as we have seen, provides part of the evidence for interpreting ἀνάμνησισ in another way, but there is the second obstacle to accepting this view of the Eucharist. The New Testament understanding of the Eucharist as sacrifice where the life and might of the Lord Jesus are released for our good is misrepresented by the presentation of this institution as only a memorial meal with a sentimental appeal.

It is the interpretation in the New Testament of the Eucharist as sacrifice which can explain why the New Testament does not associate this institution explicitly with grace. As sacrifice, the Eucharist already effected what it might be taken to effect as means of grace. We may indeed be tempted to explain the description of the Eucharist increasingly in terms of grace as due to the loss of the Biblical understanding of sacrifice experienced by Christian theology from the end of the Ancient World.

We have seen evidence in the New Testament accounts of the Last Supper and in the interpretation of it in the Synoptic Gospels, and in 1 Corinthians, that clearly presents it as a sacrifice. I have noted the efficacy of the Eucharist as conveying forgiveness of sins and eternal life, and I have inferred that its sacrificial character made it superfluous to describe it in terms of grace. Such are the grounds for thinking that in the New Testament the Eucharist is a sacrifice in Biblical terms.

Having established the character of the Eucharist, if my argument is convincing, we can now consider a further question: why did Jesus institute this observance?

The fact that Jesus and his disciples came up to Jerusalem at Passover-tide leads us to infer that they intended to celebrate the Passover together. This inference turns on Jesus' foreknowledge of his Passion and death. If he foreknew these events, he could not, on the Johannine chronology which I follow, have planned to hold the Passover. If he did not foreknow them, he seems to have been forestalled by events.

There is one other consideration, already mentioned, which implies that, whatever Jesus foresaw, he did not plan to hold a Passover. Jesus' family plays no part in the meal of Mk. xiv.12–25, and the Passover was explicitly a family occasion for which a gathering of the disciples was no substitute. If Jesus was estranged from his family in the latter part of his ministry (see my paper, 'Jesus, His Family and His Disciples' *Journal for the Study of the New Testament*, xv (1982), 3–19), he went up to Jerusalem knowing full well that, being alienated from his family, he could not hold the Passover.

In these circumstances Jesus seems to have turned to an alternative and for this there may have been positive as well as negative reasons. Not only was a family occasion such as the Passover excluded, but also Passover already had a large body of interpretations and traditions attached to it which made it in some ways an inflexible institution. On the other hand there was, as we shall see in lecture v, an observance of variable interpretation which could be, and was, made the vehicle of Jesus' purpose to a degree that was difficult for Passover.

LECTURE V

❧

The nature of the Eucharist: (2) the sacred meal

In the last lecture I concluded that in the New Testament the Eucharist was a sacrifice in Biblical terms. This was my answer to the question: is the Eucharist a sacrifice? But this question is part of a larger one: what is the Eucharist? I shall now suggest that we have to supplement our conclusion from other evidence.

You will remember that when I was looking at the theme of the food of immortality I mentioned the romance, *Joseph and Asenath* (= *JA*) as providing evidence that the expression 'bread of life' is older than and independent of John. You may have felt that I introduced this romance with too little explanation. I shall now try to make this good.

When I was considering Jeremias' interpretation of the Last Supper some twenty-five years ago, it was clear to me that it was not enough to point out the weaknesses I detected in his argument. I had to produce a convincing alternative. I must show not only that the Last Supper was not a Passover but also that it was something else.

At that time I was working on Jewish literature between the Old and New Testaments, especially as it existed in Greek. In the course of these studies I came across the romance of *JA* and I saw at once that it had been quite misunderstood. Batiffol the nineteenth-century editor had presented it as an eccentric Christian text of the fourth century A.D. This it was clearly not, but this mistaken view of the book had led to its being ignored by Biblical scholars with few exceptions.

In trying to place *JA* I noticed first the absence of specifically Christian features. The meal of initiation which, as we shall see, plays an important part in this story, has interesting resemblances to the Eucharist, but lacks its Christological character. The word μυστήριον 'mystery' used to describe this meal is employed in a way unparalleled in the New Testament.

Asenath is presented as the exemplary convert from paganism to Judaism, but there is no mention of her baptism, though we know that baptism was in first-century Judaism part of the process of admission to Israel as it was of admission to the Christian Church.

The political conditions in the story would easily reflect the state of affairs in the last century of the rule of the Ptolemies before the Roman conquest under Augustus. Egypt has its own monarch and is beset with civil disorders in which Jews are involved. The later we place *JA* after this time, the more difficult it becomes to defend our dating.

There is no trace of the programme of reconstruction under the Tannaim after 70 A.D., nothing that implies the fall of Jerusalem, nothing to suggest that Hellenistic Judaism is waning. This silence may not be very significant, but as far as it goes it favours an earlier date.

There are many links with the Greek Old Testament in vocabulary and thought. They would suggest that *JA* was nearer to the Wisdom of Solomon in thought and expression. Two key words are 'immortality' (ἀθανασία) and 'mystery' (μυστήριον). They seem only gradually to have found their way into Hellenistic Judaism, but they are both present in *JA*.

On the other hand Jewish attitudes to the Gentile mission later became more unforthcoming. Asenath, in subsequent Jewish tradition, remains the wife of Joseph, but she is no longer a pagan girl but a Jewess, the daughter of Dinah.

In all, the first century B.C. or the beginning of the first century A.D. seems the more probable time for the writing of this book. It is a piece of propaganda for the Gentile mission of Hellenistic Judaism as it can still be discerned in the Acts of the Apostles.

Asenath, the heroine of the first half of the book, has heard of Joseph, the successful administrator, and reacts against this foreign upstart. When she hears that on his tour of the province he is likely to come to Heliopolis and that her parents propose marrying her to him, she rejects the idea with scorn. None the less she falls in love with Joseph at first sight and is about to kiss him when he says:

It is not proper for a god-fearing man, who blesses the living God with his mouth and eats the blessed bread of life and drinks the blessed cup of immortality and is anointed with the chrism of incorruption, to kiss an alien woman who blesses dead and dumb idols with her mouth and eats from their table the bread of suffocation and drinks from their libation the cup of ambush and is anointed with the chrism of destruction (*JA* viii).

Asenath is distressed at this and Joseph then prays for her:

Lord God of my father Israel, the highest and mighty God, who didst quicken all things and summon them from darkness to light and from error to truth and from death to life, do thou bless this maiden also and quicken and renew her with thy spirit and let her eat of thy bread of life and drink of thy cup of blessing and number her with thy people whom thou didst choose before all things were made, and let her enter into thy rest which thou hast prepared for thine elect and let her live in thine eternal life for all time (*ibid.*).

Joseph departs and, after spending seven days in prayer and repentance, Asenath is visited by the angel Michael who says to her:

Moreover be of a good courage, Asenath, maiden and chaste one, for behold thy name is written in the book of life and shall not be wiped out for ever. But from this day shalt thou be renewed and recreated and quickened and shalt eat the blessed bread of life and drink the cup filled with immortality and be anointed with the blessed chrism of incorruption. Be of good courage, Asenath, maiden and chaste one, behold the Lord God has this day given thee to Joseph for his bride and he shall be thy husband for ever (*JA* xv).

The food of which she partakes is different from that described beforehand, but more important are the words of the angel to her:

Blessed art thou, Asenath, for the ineffable mysteries of God have been revealed to thee;

and later he says:

Lo! now thou hast eaten the bread of life and hast drunk the cup of immortality and been anointed with the unction of incorruption; lo! now today thy flesh produceth flowers of life from the fountain of the Most High, and thy bones shall be made fat like the cedars of the paradise of delight of God and unwearying powers shall maintain thee; accordingly thy youth shall not see old age, nor shall thy beauty fail for ever, but thou shalt be as a walled mother-city of all (*JA* xvi).

Judaism is here represented as a mystery, the term being used in its old classical sense, and a central observance is the religious meal. This meal serves two purposes. First, it is the occasion of initiation or admission to Judaism, and in this connexion it is significant for Asenath. Secondly, the meal of which the godly man regularly partakes seems to be sacramental, if I may use the expression.

The pattern of the meal – bread, wine and oil – differs from that of the Eucharist only in the presence of oil, but the element of interpretation is different. First, to take negative elements, there is no messianic figure involved, there is no sacrificial language and in particular no reference to blood or covenant and there is no mention of breaking the bread. Both have an eschatological reference, but the eschatological language is different, *JA*, for example, not using the expression 'kingdom of God'.

On the other hand, a blessing is said in both meals; in *JA* 'the godly man blesses the living God'. There is the contrast with the religious meals of the heathen. In 1C. x.20f there is the contrast between the cup of the Lord and the cup of demons, the table of the Lord and the table of demons. In *JA* it is the table of dead and deaf idols. In J. vi and in *JA*, as we have seen, there is the stress on the meal as conveying immortality. Both use the expression 'bread of life' and 'eternal life' and in addition *JA* talks of immortality and incorruption.

JA does not use sacrificial language. The same may be true of John as distinct from 1 Corinthians and the Synoptic Gospels. This coincidence deserves to be examined further.

In general John uses the language of sacrifice very little and in chapter vi there is only one passage which may be taken to be sacrificial: 'I am the living bread which came down from heaven. If anyone eats of this bread he will live for ever; and the bread which I shall give is my flesh on behalf of the life of the world' (vi.51). If this means that Jesus gives his life to the world, then we may have sacrificial language. This seems to be implied by the subsequent statement that 'whoever eats my flesh and drinks my blood has eternal life' (vi.54).

Those who doubt this interpretation may point out two things. First, John, unlike 1 Corinthians and the Synoptic Gospels, does not use the traditional language of sacrifice. There is nothing like the association of blood and covenant that we find in the accounts of the Last Supper.

Secondly, it may be argued that Jesus' references to giving life may rest on a vicarious transaction: I surrender life, others gain life. So we would paraphrase Jesus' words on this interpretation. On this understanding we would no more be considering a sacrifice than we would if one man stood hostage to another.

We may feel that this argument is particularly weak and that the evangelist intended by verse 51 a sacrificial statement. This being so, it seems to be the one sacrificial statement in the Eucharistic discourse, and apart from it sacrificial language seems to be lacking.

We may conclude that in the Last Supper and the meal in *JA* a basic pattern is developed partly along similar lines and partly on divergent ones. Can we find any other instance of this pattern being developed in a comparable way?

Josephus in the *Jewish War* (*B.J.* ii.119–61) written about A.D. 75–9 gives an account of the Essenes including the following particulars about their meals:

After this purification, they assemble in a private apartment which none of the uninitiated is permitted to enter; pure now themselves, they repair to the refectory as to some sacred shrine. When they have taken their seats in silence, the baker serves out the loaves to them in order, and the cook sets before each, one plate with a single course. Before meat the priest says a grace, and none may partake until after the prayer. When breakfast is ended, he pronounces a further grace; thus at the beginning and at the close they do homage to God as the bountiful giver of life (ii.129–31).

Later he writes of the novice:

Having given proof of his temperance during this probationary period, he is brought into closer touch with the rule and is allowed to share the purer kind of holy water, but is not yet received into the meetings of the community. For after this exhibition of endurance, his character is tested for two years more, and only then, if found worthy, is he enrolled in the society. But, before he may touch the common food, he is made to swear tremendous oaths (ii.138–9).

Excommunication can be fatal:

Those who are convicted of serious crimes they expel from the order; and the ejected individual often comes to a most miserable end. For, being bound by their oaths and usages, he is not at liberty to partake of other men's food, and so falls to eating grass and wastes away and dies of starvation (ii.143).

As we would expect, the texts from Qumran give a parallel to this. *The Manual of Discipline* gives the following brief account of a community meal:

And in every place where there are ten persons of the Council of the Community, let there not lack among them a man who is priest. And let them sit before him, each according to his rank, and in the same order let them ask their advice in everything.

And then when they set the table to eat, or prepare the wine to drink, the priest shall first stretch out his hand to pronounce a blessing on the first-fruits of bread and wine (1QS vi.3–5).

A longer account is given in the *Rule of the Congregation*:

And when they gather for the Community table, or to drink wine, and arrange the Community table and mix the wine to drink, let no man stretch out his hand over the first-fruits of bread and wine before the Priest; for it is he who shall bless the first-fruits of bread and wine, and shall first stretch out his hand over the bread. And afterwards, the Messiah of Israel shall stretch out his hands over the bread. And afterwards all the Congregation of the Community shall bless each according to his rank.

And they shall proceed according to this rite at every meal where at least ten persons are assembled (1QSa ii.17–22).

These texts are tantalising. They make it quite clear that the community meals perform an important function among the Essenes and at Qumran. (I distinguish between the two because, despite a manifest similarity, there are some differences between the two movements which make a total identification of the two very difficult.)

First, the meals have an initiatory character. Admission to the community meal is admission to full membership of the community. The novitiate can be understood as leading up to this condition.

Secondly, it sustains the member of the community in his membership. The excommunicate is expelled *ipso facto* from the community meal. On the other hand his sharing in the community meal is a sign of a man's continuing membership.

We have no text of the blessings over the bread and the wine. If we had, we might be able to detect the ideas that lay behind the observance. Of one point we can be sure. We cannot expect to find that the meal was understood as conferring immortality. As far as individual immortality is concerned the men of Qumran were very conservative. They believed in the continuing existence of Israel but in their own texts there does not seem to be unequivocal evidence of a belief in the survival of the individual as an individual after death.

Nonetheless the basic pattern is the same as in the Eucharist and in the meal of *JA*. A blessing of God is said over a meal of bread and wine. In the Qumran meal and probably in *JA*, the blessing is said for both bread and wine together before the meal begins, though the phrases in *JA*, 'blessed bread of life' and 'blessed cup of immortality', may be held to imply that bread and wine each had its distinct blessing of God. One difference between Qumran on one side and *JA* and the Eucharist on the other is noteworthy. In Qumran it is the priest who says the blessing.

In Genesis we have a parallel to this meal:

And Melchizedek king of Salem brought forth bread and wine: and he was priest of God Most High. And he blessed him, and said, 'Blessed be Abram of God Most High, possessor of heaven and earth: and blessed be God Most High, which hath delivered thine enemies into thy hand.' And he gave him a tenth of all (Genesis xiv.18–20 RV).

The basic elements are there, the blessing and the offering of bread and wine. There is a further contact with Qumran in that Melchizedek is a priest. If that were all, we might be tempted to assume a pattern on which the later observances of *JA*, Qumran and the Eucharist were formed.

There is, however, a difficulty. It is not surprising that Josephus and the Rabbinic texts have nothing relevant, but the older Hellenistic texts and Qumran do not help us. Some like *Jubilees* are defective at the important point in the text. Others like the *Biblical Antiquities* of Ps.-Philo almost ignore the whole passage while others again like the *Genesis Apocryphon* of Qumran merely repeat the Biblical wording.

To this silence there is one exception, the Adam and Eve literature. Some of the texts which belong to it have passages of some length devoted to Melchizedek and give some space to his offering of bread and wine. Examples are the Syriac *Book of the Cave of the Treasures* and the Ethiopic

Book of Adam and Eve. Each has Christian additions and developments, but it may be that behind these texts is an older tradition in which Melchizedek offered as priest a sacrifice of bread and wine. I cannot suggest this possibility with any great confidence, but a possibility it remains.

There is against this association of the religious meals of Qumran, *JA* and the Eucharist with the incident of Genesis xiv, the fact that none of these makes any reference to Melchizedek. As we have seen, the Qumran text requires the blessing to be said by the priest at the meal, a requirement that may be a link with the story in Genesis, but so far the Qumran material seems to have produced no association with Melchizedek for the community meal.

We have to remember in this connexion two possibilities. The first is that information more explicit about the meal may be found in new Qumran texts hitherto unpublished. The other is that careful research into the published material may yield fresh information about the Qumran meal.

I can now summarise the results of my investigation. We have three examples of a religious meal where, after the saying of one or two blessings of God, bread and wine are partaken. In all three instances they are community meals. The meal in *JA* is partaken by Israel, the people of God, in contrast to the outside world. At Qumran the meal is partaken only by members of the Qumran community in contrast with the rest of Israel and the heathen world. In the Eucharist only members of the Christian Church can partake, in contrast to all the others. Partaking in the meal is the test of membership for all instances.

Beyond this we may ask: Is any of these three observances derived from one of the others? As we have seen, the meal in *JA* and the Eucharist despite certain striking similarities have differences too great to admit of either being derived from the other.

How do *JA* and the Christian Eucharist stand in relation to the Qumran meal? We have noticed that it is most unlikely that the Qumran meal was associated with the idea of immortality, an idea that is deeply rooted in *JA* and developed in J. vi. Like *JA* the Qumran meal lacks any reference to the covenant, or any suggestion that the observance is a sacrifice. On the other hand, Qumran and the Eucharist like *JA* have a messianic theme in their interpretation of the meal, but in the Eucharist the Messiah occupies a central position in the observance, focusing the various ideas associated with it. In Qumran the Messiah of Israel seems to be present as an important member of the community, but beyond that his role seems to be obscure.

Our three examples of this kind of religious meal prove to be instances of a practice existing in Judaism at this period. They are independent of each other and develop the basic pattern of this practice, the religious meal, sometimes in the same or similar directions, sometimes with considerable differences.

Are there any other survivals of such a practice? In Rabbinic Judaism one may be detected, the sanctification of the sabbath. This is not a meal, but like the Eucharist, originally takes place at the meal at the beginning of the sabbath:

The advent of the Sabbath was marked by a 'sanctification' (*kiddush*) which set the day apart from the week-day that preceded. The head of the house, at the table surrounded by his family and guests, took a cup full of wine, pronounced over it the usual blessing (Blessed art thou, O Lord our God, King of the World, who createst the fruit of the vine) and the Blessing of the Day. Then he, and after him those seated with him at the table, drank from the 'cup of blessing'. The blessing on the bread (Who bringeth forth bread from the earth), two loaves of which were before the head of the house, symbolizing the double portion of manna on the Sabbath, followed, and the meal proceeded. (Moore, *Judaism*, II, 36)

Originally this observance took place in the house, but subsequently was transferred to the synagogue.

We noticed that in the three examples of the religious meal it served as a test of membership of the community. We find a similar state of affairs with the sanctification of the sabbath. The *Mishnah* tractate *Berakoth* (Blessings), to which I have already referred and which contains teaching of the first and second centuries A.D., has the following passage about participation:

(1) Three persons who have eaten together are bound to give an invitation. But [in the case of him who eats] suspect food and First Tithes from which their Contribution has been taken, and Second Tithes and consecrated things which have been redeemed, and the attendant who eats as much as an olive, and the Cuthaean (Samaritan) – one gives no such invitation with respect to them.
(2) But as for him who eats untithed food, and the First Tithes from which their priests' share has not been taken, and Second Tithes and consecrated things which have not been redeemed, also if the attendant eats less than as much as an olive, and the stranger – one gives no invitation with respect to them (*Mishnah Berakoth* vii).

Here the reference to the Cuthaean or Samaritan may be a survival from something older. Otherwise exclusion from participating in the Blessing has become related principally to scrupulousness and un-scrupulousness in the matter of tithing and association in the observance has become a device for encouraging the practice of tithing. We may suspect that an older practice has been developed in this direction.

If this inference is right we may see in the sanctification of the sabbath a survival of an older practice which has been applied to new purposes in the first two centuries A.D. This older practice will consist of blessings said at the partaking of bread and wine at the meal at the beginning of the sabbath in the home.

Professor Jeremias has rightly argued against the suggestion put forward by Dom G. Dix among others that the Last Supper was such an occasion. As Jeremias points out, it is not a meal nor a sacrifice nor has it sacrificial significance. It is merely the saying of a blessing. A *kiddush* (sanctification) meal has never existed if we understand by that anything other than meals at which a table grace or blessing was introduced because at the beginning of the meal the sabbath or a festival had begun. We can add to Professor Jeremias' list of differences. There is nothing messianic about the *kiddush* nor is the idea of covenant explicit in it.

Nonetheless we can add the sanctification of the sabbath, the observance of *kiddush*, to our other instances of the community religious meal in Judaism. We can now go on to ask what this practice contributed to the Last Supper.

In the main this contribution seems to have been structural. The structure, the blessing of God over bread and wine of which those present then partake, is still the structure of the Eucharist. The one addition in the Last Supper is the breaking of the bread.

As the breaking of the bread has remained a noticeable part of the Eucharist to the present time, it may be important to notice that the breaking of the bread had in early Christian tradition and interpretation nothing to do with the sufferings of Christ's body upon the cross.

A passage in John might seem to be designed to make that clear:

Since it was the Preparation, in order that the bodies should not remain on the cross on the Sabbath (for that Sabbath was a great day), the Jews asked Pilate that their legs might be broken, and they be taken away. So the soldiers came and broke the legs of the first and of the other who had been crucified with Him. They came to Jesus, and when they saw that He had already died, they did not break His legs, but one of the soldiers pierced His side with a spear, and at once blood and water came out. He who has seen has borne witness, and his witness is true, and he knows that he speaks the truth, that you too may believe. These things took place that the scripture might be fulfilled, 'A bone of him shall not be broken.' Again, another scripture says, 'They will look at him whom they pierced' (J. xix.31–7).

The expression 'break bread' is not a normal Greek one, but occurs in the Old Testament (Jeremiah xvi.7; Lamentations iv.4) and is common in Rabbinic Judaism. It is apparently no more than a practical and necessary preliminary to sharing the bread.

This being so, the addition of breaking to the account of the structure of the meal does not betoken any additional significance. We may indeed argue that it only makes explicit what is in any case implicit in the meal.

Beyond structure, the pattern of the religious meal that we have been studying does seem to be associated with one idea, that of the exclusive community. This is true as we have seen of the meal at Qumran, of that in *JA*, in the Jewish *kiddush* observance and in the Christian Eucharist, as we are reminded by words like 'excommunicate'.

This observation has an important consequence for the Eucharist. If Jesus had in mind the religious meal as the sign of membership in a community, he must have intended such a community. With this would agree the reference to covenant in Jesus' utterance over the wine. To that extent, the fact that, in all the examples we have found, the meal implies an exclusive community supports the view that Jesus intended the Eucharist as the religious meal of his society. For this reason it was an observance to be repeated.

Beyond this, the pattern of the religious meal does not seem to contribute to the ideas associated with the Eucharist. In this it stands in contrast to the category of sacrifice, to which, as we saw, the Eucharist already belongs in the Gospels and Epistles. As sacrifice, the Eucharist is the focus of many ideas. Some I have already considered. Others I shall discuss later.

Before I do this, I shall look at one structural feature in the Eucharist, the place of the Institution Narrative in the Eucharistic liturgy as we know it. I have already come near to this in my treatment of the Eucharistic Prayer and in particular in my examination of the recitation of the saving acts of the Lord as part of that prayer. I shall look further into this feature in my next lecture.

LECTURE VI

❧

The nature of the Eucharist: (3) the pattern: charter story and
ritual

In 1933 appeared a group of essays edited by the late Professor S. H.
Hooke and entitled *Myth and Ritual* (Oxford University Press). Though
it has never been reprinted, it was an influential book. One direction in
which it gave an important stimulus to further study can be inferred from
the title of its successor, also edited by S. H. Hooke, *Myth, Ritual and
Kingship* (Oxford University Press, 1958).

Though the book, *Myth and Ritual*, was so influential, it is interesting to
note that its influence seems to have been least in the subject indicated by
its title. This is true not merely of *Myth and Ritual* itself, but also of a
whole series of studies carried out under its inspiration.

S. H. Hooke himself in the first essay in *Myth and Ritual*, 'The Myth
and Ritual Pattern of the Ancient Middle East', introduced the theme
which gave the book its title. This theme is briefly that in the Ancient
Middle East there was a number of liturgical observances which had a
common pattern consisting of two parts.

After some introductory matter, S. H. Hooke introduced these two
parts or elements as follows:

To the educated reader the word 'myth' probably suggests familiar and often
very beautiful Greek stories, the themes of poet and dramatist, such as the
myths of Zeus and Semele, Theseus and the Minotaur, Perseus and the Gorgon
Medusa. But as soon as these stories are examined we find that they all contain
some thread which, like the clue which Ariadne gave to Theseus, leads back to
the centre, to the original or primitive significance of the story, to the home of the
myth. From Perseus we find a thread leading back to the Canaanite god, Resheph.
Sir Arthur Evans, in *The Palace of Minos*, has said: 'We see the Minotaur himself on the way to Crete, but if he reached the Island from the Delta, his starting-
point was still the Euphrates'. In both Dionysiac myth and ritual we find clues
pointing back to Egypt and Osiris. Hence behind the myths of Greece, in the
region of the world's most ancient civilizations, there lie those modes of behaviour which are primitive for us in the sense that they are the source of the
great body of myth and ritual characteristic of ancient culture.

When we examine these early modes of behaviour we find that their originators
were not occupied with general questions concerning the world but with certain
practical and pressing problems of daily life. There were the main problems of

securing the means of subsistence, to keep the sun and moon doing their duty, to ensure the regular flooding of the Nile, to maintain the bodily vigour of the king who was the embodiment of the prosperity of the community. There were also individual problems, how to ward off disease and ill fortune, how to acquire a knowledge of the future. In order to meet these needs the early inhabitants of Egypt and Mesopotamia developed a set of customary actions directed towards a definite end. Thus the coronation of a king, both in Egypt and Babylon, consisted of a regular pattern of actions, of things prescribed to be done, whose purpose was to fit the king completely to be the source of the well-being of the community. This is the sense in which we shall use the term 'ritual'.

Moreover, we find that these early ritual patterns consisted not only of things done but things said. The spoken word had the efficacy of an act, hence the magic value of the many punning allusions which we find in early Egyptian ritual texts, a point which will be abundantly illustrated by Dr. Blackman in his essay. In general the spoken part of a ritual consists of a description of what is being done, it is the story which the ritual enacts. This is the sense in which the term 'myth' is used in our discussion. The original myth, inseparable in the first instance from its ritual, embodies in more or less symbolic fashion, the original situation which is seasonally re-enacted in the ritual (*Myth and Ritual*, pp. 2f).

We may summarise Hooke's thesis by saying that the myth gives the origin of the ritual and provides the pattern for the ritual to follow. We may add to this the third detail that often the myth contains the command to repeat.

It is remarkable that when E. O. James, one of the contributors to *Myth and Ritual*, produced his book *Christian Myth and Ritual* (London, John Murray, 1933) he did not propound what might seem an obvious example of the myth-and-ritual pattern, the Christian Eucharist. Here the Institution Narrative would be the myth and the rest of the Eucharistic liturgy the ritual.

Why was there this failure to associate myth and ritual with the Eucharist? First, we may recall that the myth-and-ritual school from the first was interested in particular myths, for example, the myths connected with kingship, and their enactment in various observances. It may be also that the relation of myth to ritual in the pattern was not always clearly defined in the minds of the members of the group.

Secondly, the term 'myth' may itself have caused difficulty in three ways. In the first place, despite disclaimers, the word 'myth' itself may be taken as implying a judgement on the contents of the myth, that they are not historical. And in the second place, 'myth' encounters other difficulties. There is a whole debate about the nature and significance of myth of which we get an idea from G. S. Kirk's book, *Myth, Its Meaning and*

Functions (Cambridge University Press, 1970). At the moment we are far from having an answer to the problems involved, and it may seem to us that some at any rate of these problems are irrelevant to our subject.

Thirdly, the first paragraph in the extract from Hooke's essay mentions the word 'myth' and immediately proceeds to talk about Greek myths. This illustrates a widespread tendency to think of myths as principally the Greek myths, an identification that can be misleading. Unfortunately it is hard, if not impossible, to eradicate.

These three difficulties are reason enough for avoiding the term 'myth' and seeking another to take its place. The anthropologists have sometimes used the expression 'charter story' or 'charter text' and this is not open to the objections I mentioned above. From now on I shall use these expressions instead of 'myth' in my discussion.

Before we investigate further the relevance of this pattern, charter story and ritual, we may look again at some alleged Greek instances, in particular at the *Hymn to Demeter*. The *Hymn* tells the story of the carrying-off of Persephone, daughter of Demeter, by the god of the underworld. Related to this story are the Mysteries of Eleusis, and we might jump to the conclusion that *Hymn* and Mysteries are related, as charter story and ritual. If this were true, it would mean that we had a valuable clue to what took place at the Mysteries, and a striking example of the pattern we are discussing.

It is not likely to be true. Much of the Eleusinian Mysteries, as of mysteries in general, was a well-kept secret. Once we leave aside conjecture, it is remarkable how little we know of what went on. The most we can do is draw fairly clearly the line where our knowledge ends.

This can be understood from the nature of ancient mysteries. A μυστήριον, to use the Greek word, meant something into which men were initiated. It was revealed to them and withheld from all others, a secrecy strictly maintained and enforced by law at Athens for the Eleusinian mysteries.

What was this something so revealed? As far as we can make out, it consisted of objects and actions seen, and utterances and other sounds heard, all forming a body of rite and ceremony in which the initiate took part. Such a description would seem to be true of the whole class of mysteries which were enacted in the context of Greek religion.

This explains one reaction in Hellenistic Judaism which we can discern in the Wisdom of Solomon:

> For the ancient inhabitants of thy holy land,
> Hating them for doing their most detestable works of enchantments and
>   unholy rites,

> Merciless murderers of their children,
> Yea and an entrail-devourers' banquet of human flesh and of blood,
> From the midst of their mystic rite,
> And parents assassins of helpless souls
> Thou didst determine to destroy by the hands of our fathers

(xii.3–6)

and:

> For a father afflicted with untimely grief,
> Having made an image of a child quickly reft away,
> Now honoured as a god him which was then a dead human being,
> And enjoined on his dependants mysteries and initiations.

(xiv.15)

and:

> So then to err concerning the knowledge of God sufficed them not,
> But living in the midst of a great war caused by ignorance,
> They call such great evils peace.
> For enacting either rites of childmurder or secret mysteries,
> Or frenzied revels of strange ordinances,
> They keep neither their lives nor their marriages pure,
> But one either lying in wait for another slayeth him or grieveth him by
> adultery.

(xiv.22–4)

These passages show the attitude of Judaism to the mysteries understood in their classical sense as secret observances of heathenism.

In view of this reaction we can understand that Jews did not at once describe Judaism as a mystery. Philo, however, did from time to time describe Judaism in this way: 'For to reveal mysteries to the uninitiated is the act of one who destroys the laws of the priestly initiation' (*Quaestiones in Genesim* iv.8 from John Damascene, *Sac. Par.* 533). Joseph and Asenath, whose evidence I earlier found so interesting, present Judaism as a mystery cult, and the religious meal with its curious features is so described. This, however, is unusual, but it had its influence on Christianity after New Testament times. To this I shall return later.

This, however, was not the end of the story. Time and again, Hellenistic Judaism took terms out of the vocabulary of pagan Hellenism and adjusted them to the Biblical religion. The terms for 'sacrifice' (θύειν) and 'expiate' (ἱλάσκεσθαι) are examples of this.

Μυστήριον 'mystery' was such a term, but how was it acclimatised? Apparently this was done by changing the content. The content of μυστήριον is no longer a body of things seen and heard, but a divine revelation, a truth disclosed by God to his chosen and withheld from all others.

We find instances of this meaning in Wisdom. There is a noticeable difference in vocabulary between the two halves of this book. As we have seen in the second half of Wisdom, μυστήριον is used of the secret cults of paganism, but in the first half it describes the dealing of God with the righteous. The author says:

> Yea, they know not the mysteries of God;
> Neither hoped they for the reward of holiness,
> Nor recognised the prize of blameless souls,
>
> (ii.22)

and of the revelation of wisdom:

> But what wisdom is, and how she had her beginning, I will declare,
> And will not conceal from you mysteries;
> But will trace her out from the beginning of creation,
> And will bring into clearness the knowledge of her,
> And will not pass by the truth.
>
> (vi.22)

It is in this sense that the term is used in the New Testament. For example Mk. iv.11 (Mt. xiii.11, L. viii.10) 'To you is given to know the mystery of the kingdom of God' probably means 'To you is revealed the secret of the kingdom of God.' Certainly nothing is implied about a mystery cult.

Elsewhere μυστήριον comes in the Pauline Epistles, in Ephesians and 1 Timothy and in Revelation. It seems always to denote a truth that is secret from the world at large and revealed to God's chosen. In Revelation it may be translated 'secret':

i.20 The secret of the seven stars which you saw at my right hand.

x.7 God's secret was perfected as he announced to his servants the prophets.

xvii.5 On her forehead a name written Secret (μυστήριον).

xvii.7 I shall tell you the woman's secret.

Similar is the use of the word in the Epistles.

1C. ii.7 We speak God's wisdom in a revelation, hidden wisdom which God foreordained for our glory before the world, which none of the rulers of the world knew.

iv.1 Dispensers of God's revelations.

xiii.2 If I have the gift of prophecy and know all secrets and all knowledge.

73

1C. xiv.2 He who speaks in a tongue speaks not to men but to God, but in Spirit he speaks secrets.

xv.51 Behold I tell you a secret.

The same meaning appears in the rest of the Epistles. Throughout the term has this double character, a truth hidden and revealed. Nowhere in the New Testament does it refer to a cult. The use of the term, normal in paganism, for a cult secret from the outside world but revealed to the initiate, which we have seen rejected in Wisdom, used in an intellectual presentation of Judaism by Philo and embraced by *Joseph* and *Asenath*, is ignored in the New Testament and the Apostolic Fathers. Indeed, well into the second century there is no evidence that Christians called the Eucharist μυστήριον.

You may have thought that this excursus about mystery, μυστήριον, is beside the point; but my conclusion makes even more difficult the view that the Eucharist is derived from the mystery cults. At any rate the early Christians never so described it.

This, however, is not where I started. I was considering whether the Eleusinian Mysteries were an example of the pattern, charter story and ritual. We may conclude that if those Mysteries were an example of this pattern, we know nothing of it, but there are strong reasons in the nature of the Mysteries themselves why a known document, the *Hymn to Demeter*, should not be such a charter story.

We cannot deny the possibility that some of the Greek mysteries were examples of the pattern, charter story and ritual, but for the same reason as applied in the Eleusinian Mysteries, the secrecy of the observance, we have to admit that we cannot point to such examples with any confidence.

We can, however, find examples of our pattern elsewhere, and this time in the world of today. In *Essays on the Ritual of Social Relations*, ed. M. Gluckman (Manchester University Press, 1962), M. Fortes' paper on 'Ritual and Office in Tribal Society' contains an account of an observance current among an African people, the Tallensi. This observance is the focus of several themes, but among them the pattern of charter story and ritual pattern is obvious. Fortes' account of the practice is as follows:

I have time to describe only one of the simplest yet most solemn of the rites. It is, in effect, a dramatic recapitulation of the first arrival of the founding ancestor of the chiefly clans and his reception by the aboriginal Earth-priests. It takes place at night, at a sacred spot believed to be the site where these founding ancestors of the two groups lived side by side in mutual amity. On this night no-one, except those actually taking part in the ritual, is allowed out of doors. The senior Chief, as the living representative of his first ancestor, dressed in the full regalia of his office – his red hat, his rich tunic, his sandals, and his amulets – and carrying his staff of office, goes in silent procession, followed by the elders of the lineages of the clan, to the sacred site. There he and his entourage take their seats on the rock which is supposed to have been the traditional seat of the founding ancestor and his elders. Presently the senior Earth-priest arrives with his clan elders. He is also accoutred in the prescribed costume of his office, that is, antelope skins, a black string cap and official amulets, and he carries a guinea corn stalk of a variety which only Earth-priests may carry about. In the black silence, he and his followers take their seats on another rock, equally sanctified by the myth as the original seat of *their* founding ancestor.

The parties cannot see one another, for fire and light are strictly forbidden. Minutes pass in silence. Then the Earth-priest calls out, 'Speak'. An elder of the chief, in tones of profound respect, announces that the chief has come to greet the priest. Greetings are then gravely exchanged between the parties. A stranger would be bound to infer, from their manner and tone, that they had not set eyes on one another during the twelve months which have passed since they last met in this place – though, in fact, they live cheek by jowl and in daily contact. The priest asks if all the lineages of the chiefly clan are present, and if any of them is not represented he demands an explanation. This is important, since the ceremony is a reaffirmation of the original compact between the two clans, and its binding force is impaired if all branches of both clans do not participate. At this point beer and flour for the libation are handed by the chief's spokesman to the priest.

Now comes the most solemn moment. The priest begins his invocation. It is a lengthy, vivid, reverent and pious speech, addressed formally to the ancestors but in fact equally to the participants. The ancestors are adjured to attend and to receive the libation. They are exhorted to bless and prosper the people and the country so that he, the priest, and his colleague the chief, may have everlasting renown. But the principal theme of the speech is a recitation of the myth which, in Malinowski's words, constitutes the charter of the rite (pp. 76–8).

Here we have the essential features of the pattern, the charter story 'of the first arrival of the founding ancestor of the chiefly clans and his reception by the aboriginal Earth-priests' and the enactment of this event in ritual. We are not told of a command to repeat but this is clearly implied by the provision for the re-enactment of the liturgy.

Nearer home in Judaism we can find at least one example of the pattern. The Passover liturgy with its Haggada comes into mind but this does not seem to meet the conditions of the pattern. It lacks an account of the origin of the observance despite all the references to the first Passover. Nor does it give the pattern to be followed, although it explains some of the distinctive features of the ritual. In fact though it comes near to serving some of the purposes of a charter story, the Haggada is not the charter story of Passover.

This conclusion is surprising, but as the text stands in the Haggada today it seems to be unavoidable. It may be that earlier forms of the Haggada would provide instances of the pattern we seek, but this consideration underlines the fact that we still lack an adequate study of the early history of the Passover Haggada.

Our Jewish example of the pattern of charter story and ritual comes from another tradition, the tradition of the observance of the Day of Atonement in the Temple in the first century A.D. This tradition probably represents practice in the Temple in Jesus' day, and there is nothing in the tradition to suggest that the practice did not originate earlier.

The tradition is reported at *Mishnah Yoma* (Day of Atonement) vii.1–2 and in part in *Mishnah Sota* vii.7. According to *Yoma* it runs as follows:

Then the High Priest came to read. If he was minded to read in the linen garments he could do so; otherwise he would read in his own white vestment. The minister of the synagogue used to take a scroll of the Law and give it to the chief of the synagogue, and the chief of the synagogue gave it to the Prefect, and the Prefect gave it to the High Priest, and the High Priest received it standing and read it standing. And he read *After the death* . . . (Lev. 16.) and *Howbeit on the tenth day* . . . (Lev. 23²⁶⁻³².) Then he used to roll up the scroll of the Law and put it in his bosom and say, 'More is written here than I have read out before you'. *And on the tenth* . . . (Num. 29⁷⁻¹¹.) which is in the Book of Numbers, he recited by heart. Thereupon he pronounced eight Benedictions: for the Law, for the Temple-Service, for the Thanksgiving, for the Forgiveness of Sin, and for the Temple separately, and for the Israelites separately, and for the priests separately; and for the rest a [general] prayer.
2. He that can see the High Priest when he reads cannot see the bullock and the he-goat that are being burnt; and he that can see the bullock and the he-goat that are being burnt cannot see the High Priest when he reads: not that it was not permitted, but because the distance apart was great and both acts were performed at the same time (Danby's translation).

The scapegoat has been driven to the wilderness and the animals are burning on the altar when the High Priest reads or recites the three passages from the Law. These three passages give the origin of the observance, namely God's command to Moses on a particular occasion, they give the pattern to be followed and they contain the command to repeat. Thus we have an instance in first-century Judaism of the pattern, charter story and ritual, an example beyond question in contrast to the equivocal status of the Passover Haggada.

Having established the existence of the liturgical pattern, charter–ritual, in Judaism in the first century A.D., I have now to relate it to the Eucharist, but first we must notice one earlier thesis which comes near to detecting this pattern in the Christian liturgy.

We have noticed the failure of E. O. James' book, *Christian Myth and Ritual*, to consider the Eucharist in this connexion, but a step in this direction was taken by Gregory Dix in *The Shape of the Liturgy*:

THE last supper of our Lord with His disciples is the source of the liturgical eucharist, but not the model for its performance. The New Testament accounts of that supper as they stand in the received text present us with what may be called a 'seven-action scheme' of the rite then inaugurated. Our Lord (1) took bread; (2) 'gave thanks' over it; (3) broke it; (4) distributed it, saying certain words. Later He (5) took a cup; (6) 'gave thanks' over that; (7) handed it to His disciples, saying certain words. We are so accustomed to the liturgical shape of the eucharist as we know it that we do not instantly appreciate the fact that it is not based in practice on this 'seven-action scheme' but on a somewhat drastic modification of it. With absolute unanimity the liturgical tradition reproduces these seven actions as four:

(1) The offertory; bread and wine are 'taken' and placed on the table together.
(2) The prayer; the president gives thanks to God over bread and wine together.
(3) The fraction; the bread is broken. (4) The communion; the bread and wine are distributed together.

In that form and in that order these four actions constituted the absolutely invariable nucleus of every Eucharistic rite known to us throughout antiquity from the Euphrates to Gaul (p. 48).

This passage enables us to see Dom Dix moving toward my analysis of the liturgy and at the same time helps to explain why he did not discern the charter–ritual structure in the Eucharist. We must recognise that the charter narrative especially as it stands in 1 Corinthians xi represents an older stage in this particular than later Eucharistic practice, but this difference is not enough to disprove the relation of the pattern and its enactment, especially where the other features are present.

On the other hand Gregory Dix clearly discerned the basic shape or pattern of the liturgy and implied that it stood in some kind of relationship to the Institution Narratives. Much of his book is concerned, as its title warns us, with this shape or structure, with its implications and development. With great skill he prevents his study from becoming a merely formal analysis and weaves into his description of the shape of the liturgy and its history many themes of high theology.

On the other hand Gregory Dix seems not to have been aware of the charter–ritual structure. We may infer this not from his observation of the difference between the Institution Narratives and the shape of the liturgy which we noticed earlier, but from another difference which he did not notice, the absence of a command to repeat. Had Gregory Dix been aware of the significance of this, he could have used it much more effectively than he used the discordance between Institution Narrative and liturgy.

Earlier in lecture II I alluded to the fact that I Corinthians contained the command to repeat, but that it was absent from Mark, and promised a further discussion later. The time for this discussion has now come.

Had the charter–ritual pattern operated from the institution itself at the Last Supper, we would have expected the command to repeat to form an unquestionable item in the Institution Narratives. This is not so and our earlier discussion suggested that though Jesus intended that the observance should be repeated the command to repeat was introduced later.

If the charter–ritual pattern began to influence celebration of the Eucharist between the Institution and the writing of I Corinthians, it would be easy to understand the appearance of the two commands to repeat in the account in I Corinthians. The pattern required a command to repeat and the character of the Institution implied it, and so a command to repeat appeared in the tradition as Paul knew it.

It is noteworthy that on this hypothesis the command to repeat was introduced into the account in I Corinthians and not into that in Mark. In my discussion of the Institution Narrative in I Corinthians, I noticed that it showed traces of stylistic revision, which suggested a liturgical context. This consideration would agree with my hypothesis. By comparison, the liturgical influence on Mark was not so strong.

We may also notice that the account in I Corinthians had a great influence on the accounts of the Institution in later liturgies. First we notice that the Pauline account seems to have been the principal source for the distinctive matter of the longer account in L. xxii. Its influence on the account in Justin (*Apol.* i.66.3) is strong and clear. Hippolytus in the *Apostolic Tradition* depends mainly on it. The same is true of later liturgies. For example, the Latin *Canon Missae* both in the *De Sacramentis* (iv.21–2) and in the earliest liturgical manuscripts shows this dependence. There are clear marks of such dependence in another fourth-century text, the *Liturgy of Serapion*.

This predominant influence of the account in I Corinthians on later tradition is unusual in the early Church. In general it is the account in Matthew which is subsequently most used. We can see this in the quotations from the New Testament in early Christian writers from Irenaeus onward, and in the liturgical Gospels, for example in the Latin tradition. As a general rule, where Matthew provides one of a group of parallel accounts it is the Matthean account which is most used and influential.

How can we account for the exceptional place of the Pauline account in the liturgical Institution Narrative? First, as far as we know, it is the oldest account to have been put into writing and, secondly, before it was quoted in 1 Corinthians it was used liturgically, apparently in an important Christian community. This would suggest that it was widely used in the liturgy before the other accounts and, in particular, the account in Matthew were available. This precedence it seems never to have lost.

We have seen that the presence of the charter story is required in the charter–ritual pattern and this explains why, with very few exceptions, the Institution Narrative is found in all examples of the ancient Christian liturgy. Again with few exceptions it plays a threefold part in that liturgy: it gives the origin of the observance, it gives the pattern to be followed in it, and it contains the command to repeat.

This, however, does not explain why the Institution Narrative occurs in the precise place which it occupies in the Eucharistic Prayer. We may compare it with the parallel from the Day of Atonement quoted earlier from *Mishnah Yoma*. There the charter texts are not embedded in a larger whole, but stand free and distinct in the observance as a whole.

The reason for the position of the charter story within the Eucharistic Prayer seems to lie in their content. As we saw in lecture II at the discussion of *anamnesis* the core of the Eucharistic Prayer is the recital of the saving acts of the Lord from his Incarnation to his Resurrection. I suggested that already in 1 Corinthians the *anamnesis*, the proclamation of the Lord, may have contained the Institution Narrative, a reference to the death and a reference to the Second Coming. The narrative finds its place there as one of the saving acts.

This conclusion is supported by the evidence of Hippolytus. The Eucharistic Prayer in the *Apostolic Tradition* is the oldest instance of the *anamnesis*, the series of the saving acts writ large. There the Institution Narrative comes in roughly its chronological position in series. There we have in this order, Incarnation, Eucharist, Death and Passion, and Resurrection, the Eucharistic charter story in roughly its chronological position.

In this way we can explain the presence and position of the Institution Narrative in the liturgy. The Eucharist is an example of the charter–ritual pattern where the Institution Narrative is present because it is the charter story. It takes its place in the Eucharistic Prayer because it appears there in its chronological place in the saving acts of the Lord.

This explanation of the presence and position of the words of Institution in the liturgy undercuts the doctrine about these words which has been dominant in Western Christendom since the fourth century A.D., the doctrine that these words are present as constituting the factor of consecration and that the Eucharistic Prayer is built round this story, providing a theological and devotional structure enshrining the act of consecration.

If this implication is right, we shall have to take a good, hard look at some of the principles which have helped to determine the character and structure of the Eucharistic liturgy as we have known and experienced it. So far we have been discovering in various corners of our Biblical and Christian heritage, ideas and practices which may enable us to provide an alternative interpretation and liturgical pattern which is intrinsically more defensible and truer to the ideas of the Bible and the ancient Church. This I must undertake in my next lecture.

LECTURE VII

❧

The inheritance of the Eucharist and today: problems of liturgy

At the end of lecture VI we left ourselves with a problem. We had seen the Eucharistic liturgy beginning to take shape in the New Testament itself and had noted the progress of this development in the century subsequent to the New Testament. I had earlier remarked on changes in the understanding of the Eucharist in the fourth and fifth centuries and had hinted at other declensions from its older pattern and doctrine. Today we look back over some twelve years of liturgical reform and experiment. How does the product of our efforts compare with the primitive liturgy in its original significance?

Before I answer this question we should consider two preliminary assumptions. First, it is sometimes assumed that what is ancient or Biblical is automatically right. We have only to establish what the Bible says or what the ancient Church did, in order to settle the matter. For example, the liturgiologists seem sometimes to use Hippolytus in this way. The important step appears to be to recover Hippolytus' liturgy as he drafted it early in the third century, and then to re-enact as much of it as our longsuffering congregations will stomach.

Secondly, we sometimes assume that later reconstructions have a kind of divine right. Every so often we hear people talking as though the Sacramentary that Pope Hadrian sent Charlemagne or the Liturgy of Cranmer or the Tridentine Missal were normative. Each has valuable elements, each is instructive, but each has serious defects. For historical reasons the Biblical ideas and the Biblical institution are normative in a way that subsequent liturgical creation cannot be, and in gloomier moments we may feel that later liturgical developments have led us wrong more often than they have led us right.

We start, then, with the Biblical ideas and institution of the Eucharist. First, we notice that they have little to say to the first part of the historical liturgy from the salutation to the intercessions inclusive. At the ancient position of the *pax* we have a frontier, and, though we can supply threads which connect the two parts of the liturgy, they should not weaken, let alone displace, this fundamental boundary. Strictly speaking, the Eucharistic action takes place entirely beyond this boundary.

We may do well to dwell on this distinction in more detail. In the ancient

Church a series of actions clearly marked it. First, before the intercessions non-Christians in general were dismissed, and next, after the intercessions, those under instruction for baptism withdrew. Next, these external elements being removed, the faithful reconstituted themselves as the body of Christ at peace with itself by the *pax*. Then the altar was made ready, the bread and wine and other gifts were brought and put upon it, the bishop or other officiant duly washing his hands. The bishop then began the dialogue of the preface.

Already in antiquity some of the elements of this frontier were disappearing. For example, the *pax* was transferred in the West to a position at the end of the Eucharistic Prayer before the actual communion. This transference robbed the *pax* of much of its earlier significance. In due course at most Eucharists there were no unbelievers or catechumens, and so the dismissals largely fell out of use. Likewise the washing of the priest's hands disappeared in the reformed liturgies in the sixteenth century, and in general is less practised today. There has also grown up a practice of preparing the altar before the beginning of the liturgy.

The result is often a lack of awareness of this boundary between the two parts of the liturgy and of its significance. We can observe this in the uncertainty to be seen in liturgical reform today about the place in which to put the general confession and absolution. Sometimes this takes place early in the liturgy, sometimes in the position originally taken by the *pax*, and sometimes immediately before communion. Cranmer, for once, did well to put these items in the most suitable position, though we may ask ourselves how far he understood the implications of his decision, especially as he eliminated the *pax*, transferred the bringing of the offerings to before the intercessions and dispensed with the hand-washing. Nonetheless this seems to be the appropriate position. The forgiveness of sins leads naturally to the *pax* and constitutes part of the preparation for entering on the holy action. This gives us a sequence of events: the forgiveness of sins, the *pax*, the preparing of the altar and the bringing of gifts, the hand-washing and the preface, which mark, just as firmly, the transition from one part of the liturgy to another as did the ancient pattern.

I have hinted at the nature of this transition but I should now be more explicit. The first part of the liturgy was derived from the liturgy of the synagogue and had all its accessibility. The second part was a sacrificial action hedged about by all the exclusiveness of the holy, and the migration from the one to the other was a migration from the this-worldly or profane to the other-worldly or sacred.

The context of this separation thus brings us back to one of our basic themes in the Eucharist, the sacrificial action in which the life and power of the Lord are released in the holy sphere. We have just seen the concrete recognition of this holy and separate world in the observances which mark the migration into it. It is the world of God, his life and power, of the divine society and the holy action.

If I may draw together certain threads in my argument, I can now approach the issue of consecration. We saw in lecture VI that the position of the Institution Narrative in the Eucharistic Prayer was independent of any notion of consecration. I can now reinforce this argument with considerations drawn from the nature of the Eucharistic action. Like any Old Testament sacrifice it is a holy action from beginning to end. Those who enter into this action, the gifts they bring, are all *ipso facto* holy without more ado. This explains why in the Old Testament there is no act of consecration within the sacrificial action. This gives us the positive reason why there is no consecration within the Eucharistic action. If we seek a point of consecration it is at the threshold of that action both for the offerers and their offerings. We may note to Cranmer's credit that neither in 1547 nor 1552 did he speak of a prayer of consecration.

The practical consequence of this is twofold. First, the importance of maintaining the break immediately before the preface remains as great as ever. It now has the positive character of providing, in the migration from the profane to the sacred, a factor equivalent to the consecration of traditional doctrine.

Secondly, within the Eucharistic action, features of rite and especially of ceremony which had been developed under the later theory of consecration, such as exposition or elevation of the elements, should be eliminated. They represent a distortion of earlier practice which helped to undermine the understanding of the Eucharist as sacrifice in the Biblical sense.

We may notice, in this connexion, another distortion, the increasing concentration of the Eucharistic action in and round the Institution Narrative. One of the most rigorous examples of this is Cranmer's liturgy in the Book of Common Prayer of 1552. Here the actions of taking, breaking bread and communion are incorporated in the Institution Narrative. In the older practice they were understandably distributed over the Eucharistic action, a point to which I shall return.

This transportation and concentration of the so-called manual acts and the communion at the Institution Narrative does not itself make explicit the thesis that the Institution Narrative is the factor of consecration, but in fact it seems to be bound up with it as a rule and, in any case, would be congenial to it.

If the Institution Narrative is not the factor of consecration, what is it?

We have already seen the answer to two questions which between them also answer this question. The analysis of the Eucharistic action into charter story and enactment, tells us why the Narrative is there at all, and the understanding of the nature of the Eucharistic Prayer explains why the Narrative occurs precisely at the point at which it does. These considerations enable us to understand positively the function of the Narrative in the Eucharistic text without committing us to the traditional theory of consecration.

While I am discussing later teaching on consecration I may recall that often in Latin Christendom *benedicere* came in effect to mean 'consecrate'. We find it with this meaning in the *De Sacramentis* and in the *Canon Missae*. We saw in lecture I that this meaning depended on a development going away from the Biblical understanding of 'bless', inasmuch as in Biblical usage the relevant terms were confined almost exclusively to God and men.

This is the meaning intended in the instances of εὐλογεῖν in connexion with the Eucharistic Prayer, and in the contemporary liturgical forms the attempt is frequently and rightly made to make clear that the blessing is of God and not of the elements. We must, however, be alert to see that this application is carried through consistently.

We can now look at the structure, or shape, to use Gregory Dix's word, of the liturgy. This provides the following pattern: taking bread and wine, saying the prayer of blessing and thanksgiving, breaking the bread and partaking with the declaratory words. As we have seen, Dix reminded us that in one direction the pattern was soon modified. In the Institution Narrative the action with the bread and that with the cup are kept distinct, but in the liturgy they are fused together so that the taking of the elements, the thanksgiving and the partaking of each, become one action. For obvious reasons the breaking of bread has no parallel with the cup and so at this point no fusion takes place. The result is that, instead of having four plus three acts, we have only four as indicated above.

We now have the question: when did this fusion take place? In the account in I Corinthians it has not yet been effected and on one interpretation this is still true of Mark. On the other hand, in all the liturgies known to us it has already established itself. We may perhaps argue that the fusion was made in the second half of the first century, but this suggestion remains highly conjectural.

The first act in the structure is the taking of bread and wine. As we have seen, this act is performed at the end of the transition or migration from the profane to the holy, when the gifts are taken and put upon the altar. Formally, this signifies that the gifts are part of the Eucharistic action from the beginning and, as has just been said, this is important for our understanding of the place of consecration in this connexion.

It has, however, been suggested that the taking of the bread and the cup (λαβών Mk. xiv.22, 23, Mt. xxvi.26, 27, L. xxii.19, and ἔλαβεν 1C. xi.23) is not a significant action. We find a number of participle expressions in the New Testament which, it is suggested, have only narrative significance. We have, for example, instances of ἀναστάσ where it adds nothing to the narrative, A. v.17, x.23, xiii.16.

Is λαβών (ἔλαβεν) such an otiose expression? λαμβάνειν is frequently used in the LXX in a sacrificial context at the beginning of the action for the taking of the offerings: Genesis viii.20, xv.9, 10, xxii.2, 6, Exodus xviii.12, xxiv.6, 8, xxix.1 etc. It is thus the first of a series of acts that constitute the sacrificial action as a whole. This is precisely the part played by λαβών and ἔλαβεν in the Eucharistic Narrative. In this way λαβών proves to be not an otiose expression, but a term doubly justified, first because it establishes the beginning of the sacrificial action, and secondly because it locates this beginning at the end of the transition from the profane to the holy.

Our next act is the blessing and thanksgiving. Mk. xiv.22 and Mt. xxvi.26 have εὐλογήσασ in reference to the bread, and Mk. xiv.23, Mt. xxvi.27 have εὐχαριστήσασ of the cup, while L. xxii.19, 1C. xi.24 have εὐχαριστήσασ of the bread and by implication 1C. xi.25 has εὐχαριστεῖν of the cup also. We may recall 1C. x.16 'the cup of blessing as to which we say the blessing (τὸ ποτήριον τῆσ εὐλογίασ ὃ εὐλογοῦμεν)'.

If I am right in seeing a difference in content between εὐλογήσασ and εὐχαριστήσασ it would be that εὐλογήσασ refers to God's work as creator and sustainer of the universe, mankind and his people, and εὐχαριστήσασ relates to the saving acts of the Lord. As we have seen, this interpretation involves the interpretation of the two words in the light of Jewish parallels.

These verbal differences between the various New Testament accounts of the Institution are part of a series of differences which I have already discussed. The present place, however, is the one in which I should discuss these differences in relation to the liturgy of today. The practical question is: what form of the narrative should we use in the Eucharistic Prayer?

In answering this question let us assume the conclusions of the first three lectures about the New Testament accounts. According to these, the two primary sources are Mk. xiv.22–5 and 1C. xi.23–6. Where they differ, Mark is preferable at all points except for the phrase 'after supper' (μετὰ τὸ δειπνῆσαι) at 1C. xi.25. Further, the Pauline introduction, 'The Lord Jesus in the night in which he was arrested (ὁ Κύριοσ Ἰησοῦσ ἐν τῇ νυκτὶ ᾗ παρεδίδετο)', is true to fact and unexceptionable. If we accept these modifications we get the following narrative:

The Lord Jesus in the night in which he was arrested took bread and when he had said the blessing he broke it and as he gave it to them he said: 'Take, eat, this is my body.' And after supper he took the cup and after thanksgiving he gave it to them and they all drank of it, and he said to them: 'This is my blood of the covenant which is poured out for many.'

This text may seem startling in some of its details, for example in the omission of the command to repeat, but I have already argued the pros and cons of this decision. There remains only the practical issue: how are we to make such changes acceptable to a longsuffering Christian public? One important consideration is that in this as in the whole recitation of the saving acts, we are involved in an appeal to history.

I have already suggested that traces of a rehearsing of the saving acts can be seen in 1C. xi.23–6 and that by the time of Hippolytus the core of such a rehearsal is clearly to be seen in the liturgy. Further, I have argued that ἀνάμνησισ, 'proclamation', is another name for such a rehearsing.

This conclusion is important because it seems often to be assumed that the central part of the Eucharistic Prayer consists (*a*) of the Institution Narrative and (*b*) of the ἀνάμνησισ, 'memorial', of the Passion, Death, Resurrection and Ascension of the Lord, a view that is usually associated more or less consistently with the opinion that the Institution Narrative is the factor of consecration. The rest of the Eucharistic Prayer then consists largely of appropriate theological argumentation. Most Eucharistic Prayers in recent liturgical revision have this character in varying degrees. Examples of such revisions may be found in *The Alternative Service Book* (1980) (= *ASB*) and *The Book of Common Prayer* (1977, The Episcopal Church) (= *EBCP*).

We may notice that I have bypassed the beginning of the Eucharistic Prayer in my discussion. The preface is a traditional element long established. It has however no explicit counterpart in the Eucharistic Narrative, but we can establish its position in the economy of the prayer. It achieves two things. First, it makes clear the nature of that other world in which the sacred action is to take place, the world of the Lord of Hosts and of his holy people both living and departed. Secondly, and following on this presence of God and his servants, it establishes the context of worship which is so well achieved by the *sanctus*.

As the Eucharistic Prayer as a whole in Western Christendom lost its character of praise and thanksgiving, so occasional elements were developed in the preface to reintroduce something of this content. This seems to be the background of the Proper Prefaces of later liturgy. As, however, more and more of this character of praise and thanksgiving is recovered for the Eucharistic Prayer, the justification for such expansions disappears. All we need for the appropriate occasions is an indicative phrase at the corresponding place in the Eucharistic Prayer. For example, at Christmas we could have something as follows: 'who, as at this time, became man' etc.

We may now return to the main course of the Prayer. I have argued that this consists of blessing God for our creation and preservation and of thanksgiving for the saving acts of the Lord. We may give these in greater detail as consisting of the following: the Nativity, the Ministry, the Passion including the Institution Narrative, Death, Resurrection and Ascension. To these might be added the outpouring of the Spirit at Pentecost and an eschatological reference, 'until he come', already present in 1C. xi.26.

Before I discuss this last item further, we may notice that the content of the blessing and thanksgiving together correspond to the bulk of the Creeds. We remember that the recitation of the Creed is a relative late comer to the liturgy, being introduced in the West long after the Eucharistic Prayer had changed its character. If the older content and structure is restored to the prayer, the use of the Creed needs serious consideration. This is not a call to eliminate it from the liturgy, but to avoid what might become vain repetition.

Let us now return to the eschatological reference of 1C. xi.26. We have seen that in addition to this reference there are Jewish parallels to an element of petition at this point. How far should they be developed?

Certain elements seem to belong here, for example the petitions which are immediately relevant to the Eucharistic action, namely that our offering should be acceptable and should be for us and for all who partake the body and blood of the Lord. Beyond that we have the statement of eschatological expectation.

Far and wide in the ancient Church this modest element was developed into a large mass of intercessions, which had two principal consequences. First, these intercessions competed with the traditional prayers of the Church following the sermon. They probably were one of the factors that led to the disappearance of these prayers, a development which, among other things, led to the loss of the congregational character of the intercessions. This happened because in the Eucharistic Prayer all was said by the celebrant.

Secondly, as the element of the intercession in the Eucharistic Prayer was expanded, it led to a destruction of the balance of that prayer and a substantial change in its character. Concretely, as the element of blessing and thanksgiving was severely contracted, so the intercessions in their expanded form characterised the resulting form of the prayer. This can be clearly seen when we mark how intercession of one kind or another dominates the classical form of the Latin *Canon Missae*.

The plan of the Eucharistic Prayer that most fits in with the indications of the New Testament and Jewish practice contemporary with it, is as follows: first come the dialogue and the preface, which introduce us to the divine society within the holy sphere and establish the context of worship; secondly there are the blessing of God for creation and preservation and the thanksgiving for the saving acts of the Lord; thirdly there are the statement of the eschatological expectation and the Eucharistic petitions; and fourthly there is the formal liturgical end of the prayer. This last we have not previously discussed, but it continues an old tradition, though there is no clear reference to it in the New Testament.

At this point in the fourth and fifth centuries the Lord's Prayer was added in East and West. It is at first sight surprising that the Lord's Prayer did not earlier form part of the Eucharistic liturgy, but when we examine its content our surprise is abated; the clause, 'give us this day our daily bread', alone seems immediately relevant. Other petitions would come more happily at the end of the Church's intercessions, and some recent liturgical revisions have very successfully transferred it to this place.

This transference takes account of another consideration. We know that Christians in the ancient Church came to think it unfortunate that the liturgy lacked the Lord's own prayer and this seems to have been one argument in favour of its introduction in the fourth and fifth centuries. In this connexion it is interesting to note that we have no evidence of its being attached to the end of the intercessions, a place which would seem to be intrinsically most suitable. Part of the explanation may be that already the Church's intercessions were on the way out.

The next two items, the breaking of bread and the partaking of the elements, require little explanation. As we have seen, the attempts in various liturigcal forms to attach these acts immediately to the Institution Narrative led to a distortion of the whole Eucharistic action and recent revisions have been successful, for the most part, in restoring them to their original position.

The words of distribution are dependent on the declaratory statements in the accounts of the Last Supper. Inevitably they are a modification of these statements required by the change in context. The celebrant does not speak the words of Jesus as Jesus. 'This is my body, this is my blood', become 'The body of our Lord Jesus Christ, the blood of our Lord Jesus Christ'.

There is one further development already foreshadowed in the New Testament. As we have seen, J. vi identifies the Eucharistic elements with the food of immortality, a theme which is continued after New Testament times. This identification seems, in many quarters, to have been taken up into the words of administration in Latin, English and other languages. The words of the Prayer Book, for example, 'The body of our Lord Jesus Christ, which was given for thee, preserve thy body and soul unto ever-lasting life', retain this association, which was lost in the speedy, 'The body of Christ', e.g. *ASB* 143.

To my mind the ancient liturgy ended abruptly. The Latin Missal, with its 'Ite, missa est', preserved this abruptness until modern times. It can be understood if we recall that the ancient Church thought of the Eucharist as a sacrifice and once the sacrifice was completed it was at an end without more ado. In this way, what seems abrupt to us, who are used to con-ventional liturgical endings, was not abrupt to earlier Christians: the sacrifice had reached its appointed end.

I notice, in modern attempts to conform the end of the liturgy to what we might nowadays expect, an unsureness of touch. Ending is alternative to ending and it is possible to pile one on top of another like Pelion on Ossa. It may be that this unsureness has deeper roots, but its consequences are clear in the liturgical suggestions for the ending.

I may be able to put my finger on one of the reasons for this uncertainty. We saw that at the beginning of the Eucharistic action the Christian com-munity was reconstituted as the body of Christ and made the migration from the profane to the holy world embarking on the sacred action. The paradox is that it enters and re-enters this holy world but never leaves it. Any suggestion that we do leave it, that we are dismissed from it, that we go out into the world away from the holy gathering, must ring false and leave us with a feeling of dissatisfaction. The sacrifice may be completed but we do not depart from the sanctuary; cf. *ASB* 199, 200.

We may notice one other feature of ancient usage. We know that the anthems, gradual and alleluya or tract, belong to the primitive stage of Christian worship, but the other anthems, *introit*, offertory and com-munion were introduced in the ancient Church but at a later date. Ac-cordingly there was no element of hymns or anthems constituting a normal part of the liturgy after the lessons. This does not mean that they are out of place, but that as a later development they are not directly affected by our inquiries.

The singing of parts of the liturgy, for example, the preface, is much older. It differs from the anthems in that the texts concerned are not an adventitious element, but belong to the structure of the liturgy as far back as we can trace its wording. We may draw an important conclusion from this fact. The singing of appropriate parts of the text is in order, but the content of the texts must be appropriate. They must not clog the action of the liturgy or lead to developments that alter its emphasis or direction. As an example of this we have the Lord's Prayer at the end of the Eucharistic Prayer, which itself generates in the West an extension of its clauses in the prayer 'Libera nos' ('deliver us'). This reinforced the petitionary element already too largely developed at this point of the liturgy.

If we have supplementary texts such as the communion anthems or other items from Scripture, we can help to reduce this danger in two ways. First, we must choose material that is in keeping with the liturgical context and, secondly, we prevent any one item from dominating its context by varying the items. This was one advantage of the traditional communion anthems; they varied from day to day and so no one of them exercised a strong influence on the liturgy.

We may now consider two departures from the original practice which concern the Eucharistic elements. First, in the original Institution the bread was broken, but in modern usage more often than not each participant receives a wafer which, throughout the Eucharistic action, remains a distinct unbroken whole. In fact, for the most part it seems to be accepted as normal that the faithful receive such unbroken wafers. *ASB* 142, 196, *EBCP* 337, 364 imply that the bread is broken. The 'implication' is not always observed.

This is unfortunate in that it weakens our sense of the social significance of the whole action. It is so easy for the individual to adopt the attitude shown by the phrase, 'make my communion', a phrase which indicates a stress on the individual which is quite out of keeping with the whole Eucharistic action, where the individual is significant in and through his membership in the body of Christ. The one bread which is broken reminds us of this, whereas an unbroken wafer with its continuous separate existence does not.

The second departure consists in the reservation of the Eucharistic elements. Biblical practice was firm and clear that the sacrificial elements were confined to the holy area and not kept after the day of sacrifice. This can be seen in the rules about Passover, for example: 'You shall slaughter from the flock, or from the herd a Passover victim to the Lord your God in the place which he will choose as a dwelling for his Name' (Deuteronomy xvi.2), and 'You shall not leave any of it till morning; if anything is left over until morning, it must be destroyed by fire' (Exodus xii.10). It is not to be kept to the next morning and the Passover action takes place only in the hallowed area (cf. *Mishnah Pesahim* for the Mishnaic practice).

Already in Corinth we encounter a different state of affairs (1C. x.25). Apparently sacrificial meat may be bought in the meat market and consumed anywhere. This pagan practice stands in sharp contrast to what we find in the Bible. There are traces of a more restricted practice in Roman religion but quite clearly restrictions had broken down at Corinth in the first century A.D.

Christians in the first century had no geographical holy area corresponding to the Temple at Jerusalem. Hence rules such as those we detect in the Old Testament and the *Mishnah* do not operate for the Christian community. The Eucharist, the Christian sacrifice, could in principle be performed anywhere. This disposed of the restriction to place.

The restriction to time likewise does not seem to have obtained. By the second century A.D. Christians were certainly practising the reservation of the Eucharistic bread and, from then on, this usage has been continuous. Under various conditions it is now widespread in Christendom.

We notice two characteristics of reservation. First, it almost always took place in a church under strict control. This seems to have been true as soon as Christians had distinctive church buildings. Hippolytus mentions strict regulations for the protection of the Eucharistic elements (*Apostolic Tradition* xxxii.2) and we may assume that he is here reporting established practice.

Secondly, the Eucharistic elements, especially the Eucharistic bread, admitted more easily of preservation than the flesh of many Old Testament sacrifices. We do not suggest that the danger of rapid corruption was the reason for Old Testament practice, but the absence of such a danger made reservation more acceptable for the Christian sacrifice.

In recognising a departure from Biblical custom at this point, we notice that in older Christian practice the elements reserved become effective only in a Eucharistic context, and, when the Eucharistic context is not re-created by enacting appropriate parts of the Eucharistic liturgy the elements are definitely held back from profane access and usage. This looks very much like an attempt to maintain the principle of much Biblical practice, that a sacrifice is performed only in the holy area. The Christian tradition has always been concerned to preserve this.

At this point we may notice another post-Biblical development, the intrusion of an *epiklesis* of the Holy Spirit into the Eucharistic action. This can be explained in part as an attempt to remedy a lack in the primitive accounts, the failure to mention the Spirit as having a share in the Eucharistic action. We can try to understand this as being a result of the fact that the Eucharist was understood exclusively as a sacrifice and in this way represented a more primitive way of thinking than we find either in the doctrine of the sacraments or the *epiklesis* of the Holy Spirit. The references to the operation of the Holy Spirit, *ASB* 191 etc., *EBCP* 363, 369, are unfortunate.

The doctrine of grace as we find it in the Pauline Epistles, for example, is a relatively new thing, but the Pauline doctrine of the Spirit rests on older foundations. Nonetheless, we may notice that the New Testament doctrine of the Eucharist seems to be independent as much of the doctrine of the Spirit as of the doctrine of grace. We may recognise that within its limitations the doctrine of grace is a legitimate mode of describing certain aspects of the Eucharist and, in the same way, we may wish to see the Eucharistic action in relation to the Holy Spirit as described in the New Testament.

It is when we try to see the *epiklesis* in this light that we run into difficulties. The *epiklesis* is the Invocation of the Spirit on the elements of bread and wine. It is traditionally made after the recitation of the saving acts of the Lord, and is immediately concerned to effect the consecration of the bread and wine as the body and blood of the Lord. Orthodox theologians will quickly point out that the *epiklesis* is not the exclusive factor of consecration but the climax of a process; according to this understanding the whole Eucharistic Prayer is consecratory.

We may detect here two layers of thinking, the older more conformable to the Biblical notion of sacrifice, according to which there is not a precise moment of sacrifice, and a later in which the *epiklesis* of the Spirit is in practice the factor of consecration. Though the *epiklesis* does not seem ever to have been associated in Eastern Christianity with the cultus of the elements, yet, as far as it is regarded as the factor of consecration, it has come to occupy in Eastern theology a position corresponding to the Institution Narrative in Western liturgy as the factor of consecration.

It suffers from the same weakness. First, the Bible knows nothing of it, as it knows nothing of a factor of consecration within the Eucharistic action. This is not final but it should serve notice on us that we must find good and sufficient reason to justify this development.

Secondly, it conflicts with the Biblical idea of sacrifice. This, as we have seen, provides for a consecration, not in the course of the sacrificial action but at the beginning, when the holy action is begun within the holy area. This positive conflict with what we find in the Bible is much more serious than any lack of Biblical warrant.

Thirdly, not merely does it disconnect the consecration of the elements from the idea of sacrifice, but it tends to secularise the preceding parts of the Eucharistic Prayer. The preface, the blessing of God for our creation and preservation, the thanksgiving for the saving acts of the Lord, all precede the climax of consecration.

Fourthly, consecration by the descent of the Spirit is not perhaps the best ground for interpreting Eucharistic consecration. What the New Testament implies, as the ground of our doing what we do, is the covenant. By virtue of this and our Lord's Institution, we celebrate the Eucharist in the belief that thereby we do what is well-pleasing to God and healthful to men. The *epiklesis* can become a factor which seems to render all this otiose.

If the *epiklesis* is an unfortunate development in the association of the Spirit with the Eucharist, how can this be better achieved? for undoubtedly the Orthodox are right in regarding the New Testament accounts as archaic and incomplete in this respect. We may do well to start again from Scripture. There is first the association of the Spirit with the work of creation and inspiration. Next there is the part of the Spirit in the offering of Christ: 'how much more shall the blood of Christ who through the eternal Spirit offered himself without spot to God, cleanse our consciences' etc. (H. ix.14). Again, we can add a reference to Pentecost at the end of the saving acts, and the Spirit comes in this clause. Between them these additions would help to remedy the defect that Eastern Christians find in the traditional Western liturgy. Further developments on the same lines may establish themselves, but we must, in accepting them, preserve the balance in the content of the liturgy.

We have surveyed the principle features of the Eucharistic action as indicated in the New Testament accounts and explicit in the earliest evidences of Christian liturgy. We have noticed various attempts to recover something of this liturgical pattern. The liturgies we have inherited have, at various points, strayed far from it, and our present attempts to re-establish what is valuable in older practice do not always seem well-informed.

One difficulty in such attempts is caused by a desire to be ecumenical, for example, to establish contact with Orthodox or Roman liturgical practice. We have seen one example of this in references to the operation of the Holy Spirit as a factor in consecration (p. 191). The regrettable intrusion into the Eucharistic Prayer, 'Christ has died: Christ is risen: Christ will come again' (*ASB* 141 etc.) with its suggestion that Christ is not with his Church during the liturgy seems to be an example of this. Indeed, we may suspect that wherever a liturgical innovation appears to be faulty we have to do with an ill-judged imitation of a contemporary liturgy.

Our attempts encounter another difficulty. When I was a boy I was taught that the Holy Communion service had the following focal points: confession and absolution, offering, consecration, communion and thanksgiving. When we compare this with the pattern: taking, thanksgiving, breaking, partaking, we can see how big a revolution in devotional habits we are demanding of our fellow Christians in any attempt to substitute one pattern for the other.

First, we notice that this attempt is an attempt to return to history. The pattern in which I was brought up as a boy departs from the earliest forms of the tradition in several obvious and serious features, where there is no reason for thinking that this departure represents what happened as adequately as the primary accounts. In short, I was brought up to something that, in many ways was far from what Jesus did and intended, if our earliest sources are right.

We have already noticed some of the differences in detail. For example, the appearance of consecration as in some ways the climax of the action, perverted the whole action, and communion itself could easily become an optional adjunct to this main event. The shift of thanksgiving from the central prayer to a final position as a kind of appendix reflected the Eucharistic Prayer's loss of its character as a thanksgiving.

The disappearance of the Biblical understanding of sacrifice in favour of an artificial reconstruction, and the creation and development of the idea of sacrament, had two consequences.

(*a*) There was a change in the relationship of God to the liturgical action. In primitive sacrificing God was often the recipient or one of the recipients of the offering. This included the material offerings as well as praise and prayer. The Israelites however, were soon taught that God had no need of material food. We have already seen some of the stages by which this conviction was reached in the Old Testament. It is stated in such passages as Psalm l.13 'Shall I eat the flesh of bulls or drink the blood of goats?'

This development created a problem. We can divide early sacrifices into those in which God was a participant and those in which he was not. At the same time we may notice a tendency to give all sacrifice a Godward reference. This stands in contrast to the other tendency to eliminate God's participation in the materials of sacrifice. How were these two developments to be reconciled?

The Old Testament had already arrived at an answer to this question as we can see from the next verse in the Psalm quoted above: 'Offer to God the sacrifice of thanksgiving and pay your vows to the Most High' (Psalm l.14). The idea is carried further in Psalm xl.6–8 'If thou hadst desired sacrifice and offering thou wouldst have given me ears to hear. If thou hadst asked for whole-offering and sin-offering I would have said, "Here I am." My desire is to do thy will,

O God, and thy law is in my heart.' We can see from this that, instead of the offering to God of material sacrifices, he is offered the praise and thanksgiving of the worshippers and their giving of self and service to do his will. In this way divine participation is secured in the changed understanding of what God does or does not seek in sacrifice.

If we apply this to the Eucharist we can see the further development of these ideas. The blessing and thanksgiving are essential elements in the offering to God. They are in the tradition of sacrifice and, at the same time, commemorate the Son's offering of himself to do the will of the Father (H. x.5–9 quoting Psalm xl.6–8). This is a second element in securing the divine participation.

This offering of self to do God's will has an important bearing on our part in the Eucharistic action. The Son offers himself and we as members of his body offer ourselves in him. This has a bearing on the offering of the bread and wine. We may recognise at once that God no more needs of us bread and wine than he does the flesh of bulls or the blood of goats; but they are offered as the body of Christ, the tokens of his offering of himself in which we are involved. In this way God can and does still enter into the action as participant and we take part in it as offerers in and through Christ. This interpretation makes it clear that these ideas must be represented in the liturgy and that the elimination of the notes of praise and thanksgiving from most of the Eucharistic Prayer distorted the whole action.

(*b*) The second consequence resulting from the disappearance of the Biblical understanding of sacrifice and the advancement of the idea of sacrament, was social and cultic. The institution of sacrifice usually had a social character. There were in the Old Testament the sacrifices of individuals, but, for the most part, they are the offerings of groups and the sacrificial process as it developed made it more and more difficult for it, in any circumstances, to remain an individual affair. In contrast, as we have already noticed, if I 'make my communion', I may even in the company of others be engrossed in a private and individual concern. I am present with others just as a matter of convenience. This stress on making my communion as a means of grace indicates the defect of the definition of a sacrament in these terms. Thanks to it we can easily arrive at the notion that it is a means of grace and nothing else.

This emphasis on the means of grace also lacks a reference to worship. The Eucharist continued to be an act of worship but the doctrine of grace in the sacrament encouraged men to put the stress elsewhere; worship tended to be associated more and more with consecration.

The remarkable thing was that, despite the loss of the Biblical notion of sacrifice and the dominance of that of sacrament, so much of the wider character of the Eucharist survived.

As we have seen, ancient sacrifice usually had a social aspect, it involved offering and worship and it issued in the release of extraordinary life and power for the welfare of all who duly partook. These characteristics, which maintained themselves in a weaker form, gain in force and effect once the distorting consequences of subsequent developments are removed.

When we look at recent revisions of the liturgy we notice that something of these values has been recovered. Formally, thanksgiving has returned in various degrees to the Eucharistic Prayer, which has become again much more the prayer of thanksgiving. Correspondingly the adventitious prayers of thanksgiving after communion have either been dropped or at least weakened. This has led to an expansion of the worship throughout the liturgy instead of its concentration at certain points. The social character of the action has likewise received greater emphasis and the re-establishment of community features and congregational participation have helped to combat the concentration on the individual that we sometimes encountered in the traditional liturgies.

Nonetheless we notice an uncertainty, a lack of sureness of touch, in handling the doctrinal issues. For example, the medieval doctrine of sacrifice has been widely discredited, but there has been no corresponding return to the Biblical notion of sacrifice, with the result that sacrifice, as a whole, has often ceased to be a significant notion in recent liturgies. In this way the Eucharistic Prayer, for example, still sometimes seems to be a somewhat disjointed production. We have a feeling that we do not really know where we are going.

I mentioned earlier an attempt to return to history. Our revisions seem sometimes to be halfhearted over this. One example already mentioned is the Institution Narrative. Another is the Lord's Prayer.

We may argue that only those parts of the Lord's Prayer which occur in both Matthew and Luke can be ascribed with any confidence to Jesus. Beyond this no clause which does not occur in the original text of Matthew or Luke has any claim to be genuine. Thus the doxology, 'For thine is the kingdom, the power and the glory for ever and ever', does not occur in Luke and is not part of the original text of Matthew. Yet many modern revisions introduce with the words 'As our Saviour Christ has commanded and taught us we are bold to say' the Lord's Prayer as it stands in Matthew followed by the doxology.

It is noteworthy in this connexion that the makers of the modern liturgies for the greater part do not seem to have tried to find out what the nature of the basic notions such as Biblical sacrifice are. We may associate this with the lack of concern for historical accuracy in such details as those mentioned above. It may be part of a readiness to think of the Eucharist as something of a fairy tale which has come down from the past, in which accuracy in ideas and in details is not to be too closely sought after. This attitude is not of course explicit but can be inferred from what the liturgical revisers have done from time to time.

We have behind this of course the question: how far is the idea of sacrifice in itself a valid and relevant notion? This question takes us beyond my present inquiry to larger issues, which I must examine in the next lecture.

LECTURE VIII

❧

Conclusion

We have seen that, while the Godward reference was not originally present in all sacrifices, gradually it was extended to cover most of them until at last sacrifice might be described as an institution at home in the meeting of God and man. Further the beneficiaries of sacrifice, if so we may call them, were, to start with, gods, men and things, but in due course the benefits of sacrifice were confined to God and men. Things, material objects, played a part only as accompaniments of the traffic from men to God. While they were never eliminated, they formed a less and less significant element in the exchange between God and men. More and more the items of exchange were, from the side of God, life and power, and, from men, the offering of praise and worship.

In general terms these are basic ideas in the more developed forms of sacrifice. While we can still detect in the Old Testament more primitive notions, they do not detract from the basic idea that sacrifice is involved in the meeting and exchanges of God and men. We recognise, of course, that this is mainly what religion is about, but we have also to recognise that within this meeting or exchange between God and men are institutions and practices which give concreteness and definition to it. We can gain some idea of the nature of the institutions by listing some of them: in addition to sacrifice, the divine society, initiation, prophecy, Holy Scripture, are examples; each has its distinctive doctrine which yet has certain things in common with others.

Sacrifice like them assumes the primacy of God, and obviously they arise out of God's initiative. Thus God forms the divine society and calls man into it, he inspires the prophets and speaks through Scripture. Man is involved in these institutions, but while he co-operates with God he does so in response to the divine initiative. Sacrifice on the other hand does involve both God and man, but at first sight, at any rate, the initiative seems to rest with man; he offers to God, who receives and gives again.

Despite the superficial attraction of this view of sacrifice it ignores certain conditions presupposed by the institution. They can clearly be seen in the story of Jacob at Bethel. This story does not begin but ends with sacrifice, and the sacrifice, the anointing of the stone with oil, is

Jacob's reaction to what has gone before. Jacob has a vision of God in his dream at Bethel and then the story continues:

Jacob woke from his sleep and said, 'Truly the Lord is in this place, and I did not know it.' Then he was afraid and said, 'How fearsome is this place! This is no other than the house of God, this is the gate of heaven.' Jacob rose early in the morning, took the stone on which he had laid his head, set it up as a sacred pillar and poured oil on the top of it. He named that place Bethel; but the earlier name of the city was Luz.

Thereupon Jacob made this vow: 'If God will be with me, if he will protect me on my journey and give me food to eat and clothes to wear, and I come back safely to my father's house, then the Lord shall be my God, and this stone which I have set up as a sacred pillar shall be a house of God' (Genesis xxviii.16–22).

In this way sacrifice comes into line with the other institutions. In initiation, for example, all that man does is in response to the call from God into the divine society. This is as true of baptism as of the Old Testament practice, though if we went by what met the eye only we would assume the human initiative.

We may notice that at Bethel the story is not one of simple reaction, important as this is. In the vision God promises the land to Jacob's descendants, and with it protection and blessing such as all nations shall aspire to: 'All the families of the earth shall pray to be blessed as you and your descendants are blessed' (Genesis xxviii.14). Jacob, as we have seen, looks to God for protection and provision on his journey. God promises, man accepts the promise and offers worship in return. Man's reaction is not just to God's presence but to God as present and providing for man's welfare.

We see this made just as concrete in the Christian Eucharist. This is a reaction not only to the presence of God but to God's manifestation of himself in the saving acts of the Lord. Beyond this we have a specific act of the Lord which serves and, as we have argued, was intended to serve as a pattern to be followed by the faithful. This manifestation of the saving and prospering power of the Lord calls forth from man a response whose precise nature has been determined by what Jesus did.

This last point is important; Jesus is the pioneer of the Eucharist. He first offers himself in love and worship to the Father, and in him and through him we continue this offering. Against this stands the work of God as creator and sustainer and maker of the promises.

We may then see the Eucharist as generically an occasion of the meeting of God and man in which the manifestation of God as creator, sustainer and redeemer provokes a reaction from man.

Once the primacy of God is recognised in the Christian sacrifice we may go on to consider the nature of the exchange that takes place in this meeting of God and man. Here we may recognise at once that the various occasions of such meetings have a common character which has been most thoroughly explored in the Christian doctrine of grace.

I shall not repeat this doctrine as a whole, but I shall notice one or two features which are relevant to my exploration. Grace is a term describing God's action on man for his salvation and welfare. While God retains the initiative, his action respects man's nature; man is not treated as a thing. The language of compulsion would be alien to this intercourse, but terms like 'influence' and 'persuade' are in keeping with it. The nearest analogy seems to be the intercourse between man and man where each respects the other.

On the other hand, grace implies a real dependence by man on God. This dependence is illustrated by the whole history of the relations between God and man. It implies two things, man's continual need and God's ability to meet that need. We can understand all that comes to man from God in sacrifice in these terms.

What however are we to say of man's offering to God in sacrifice? At this point we are compelled to realise that the partners in the exchange are not on the same level. God in sacrifice does not reveal a continuing need nor does man of himself have any ability to meet such a need if it existed. What then are we to say of man's response to God in worship?

Here we meet the basic difficulty in any attempt to describe what worship is. If we cannot describe it in terms of God's need or of man's giving something to God which he does not already have, how are we to describe it? We must answer that we do not see a way of doing this adequately.

We can however achieve a partial description by considering the human aspect. First, we have the analogy of human relationships. Man is committed to a social life and this involves various kinds of exchanges, exchanges that are conditioned by the fact that men are in these exchanges in a condition of equality.

The exchanges with God are partly similar and partly dissimilar; similar inasmuch as they too can be described as social, dissimilar inasmuch as God and man are not on an equality, though God does respect the personality of man in these exchanges.

We may illustrate this from Scripture. God speaks through man to man. The precipitate of this is the Bible, but whereas God can and does speak through the Bible, we cannot identify him with the Bible. As we have seen, the Bible is a vehicle of the Word of God, but not the Word of God itself. Very roughly we may distinguish between the message, what God has to say, and the medium through which it is conveyed.

Can we say anything more about the medium? First, there are the limitations of the human context. Thus we detect the limitations of a people living in Palestine in the period before Christ and in the Graeco-Roman world in the first century A.D., economic, social, cultural, political and religious limitations. Beyond this we can detect positive error, a view of the world which is not only limited but also mistaken.

Can we detect in the human contribution anything which is not limited and mistaken? If we do not assert that when God wrote the New Testament, out of the unlimited variety of styles of which he was master he chose some dozen to use in these books, we may regard the several styles we can discover in the New Testament as proper to the human authors and as not being limited and mistaken. They are a resourceful means of presenting the Christian message. The gifts of style and conception which we find in these books can be best understood as characteristic of the several authors. To that extent we may think of the human authors as making a positive as well as a negative contribution to the formulation of the New Testament message.

In making this distinction we do not pretend that a nice separation can always be made of the human and the divine, but only that we can recognise in principle a human as well as a divine element in Scripture. This recognition should help us by analogy to understand certain aspects of worship.

Thus we can perhaps comprehend a little more clearly the part that God and man can play in worship. There is the manifestation of God in his saving and upholding power and there is man's response to this. This response has a great range of possibilities before it and we can see the exploration of many of these responses in the various forms of historic liturgy.

We can detect in liturgy, as in Scripture, traces of human limitation and error. Language, for example, can prove to be a limiting factor in worship. I am not as at home in spoken Spanish as in Latin, and consequently when I hear the Eucharist in Spanish I depend on those elements of the Spanish text which are much the same as in Latin. When I hear 'libera nos' I know where I am. Again we can sometimes see in various liturgies of the past the expression of views which now seem mistaken.

On the other hand liturgy can, and should be, a creation of great beauty. If we take the medieval Latin liturgy, we can see it as a part of a great artistic whole made up of texts, music, action, setting and architecture. On occasion the impact of this whole must have been tremendous, and that despite elements of medieval liturgy which must have provoked our dissent.

We may at this point take time off to comment on one aspect of modern rewriting of the liturgy. It has been conditioned by various migrations, the migration from Latin to the vernacular and the migration, for example, from essentially sixteenth-century to modern English. Such migrations are justifiable, but it sometimes seems as though the modern revisers have been so occupied with migrations of this kind and with changes of substance that the aesthetic quality of liturgy has had by comparison short shrift.

This is understandable. A liturgical commission may be given its mandate of revision and told to come back in two years time with material for legislation. By contrast we know from his various published drafts and liturgical texts that Cranmer was working for years at their language. If we praise the English of Cranmer's liturgy, we must not forget the years of toil that went into its making. We may get the impression that no comparable labour is to be spent on the liturgical texts of today and that we shall be left with a liturgy that is sometimes very rough-hewn for a long time to come.

I mention the aesthetic aspect of liturgy not as in any sense an explanation of worship but as something contributing to this exchange between God and man. Worship is not just an aesthetic exercise, and any attempt to make it one will frustrate its real purpose.

Worship is then an exchange between God and man in which God has taken the initiative. It is much more than that, but that will suffice for the moment. Yet we must not forget that, even in man's response to God, God has prepared the way. He has created man with all his responsibilities, his gifts and powers, the ability to respond to God in the meeting between God and man.

The Eucharist has the generic characteristics of worship, but is specifically much more. We can gain some idea of the difference by comparing the Eucharist with the offices, Matins and the rest. These are already moderately developed providing occasions not only of worship but also of instruction, but by comparison with the liturgy they are a much more jejune affair. They do, of course, by assumption and allusion, involve much of Christian theology, but, time and again, what is assumed and alluded to in the offices becomes explicit in the Eucharist.

Let us start with a concrete difference. The Eucharist contains the foundation story, the Institution Narrative, which it proceeds to enact. As we have seen, this involves an appeal to history to which there is nothing comparable in the offices. We may however bring the offices into touch with such an appeal by remembering that the Eucharist also includes the proclamation of God's dealings with man in history. Sometimes the offices imply something of this proclamation, sometimes they are more explicit, but the appeal to a particular event in history as fundamental still distinguishes the Eucharist from them.

We have already seen that the manifestation of God at Bethel is a manifestation of a god of power and promise. As such Jacob accepts and worships him. In the Eucharist God is worshipped as creator and sustainer, redeemer and hope of man. He has done and will do great things for us. It is this manifestation of God as the God of power and love and promise, who has done great things and will do greater for us in time to come, who calls forth our worship.

It is as recipients of the manifold goodness of God that we are empowered to do this. We declare that we have been called into the divine society, into membership of the body of Christ and so are heirs of all the promises made to the divine society in the past. God has redeemed us, re-established us and given us the strength and understanding required in our response.

This response, our praise and thanksgiving to God for all the benefits we have received from him and from his Son, is contained in the Eucharistic Prayer. In this way our response to God in worship not only is directed to God but has its content provided by him.

As we have seen, part of this response is offering. Again we act as members of the body of Christ and our offering is taken up in his. He offered himself to do the will of the Father for us men and for our salvation. We as members of him offer ourselves in praise and thanksgiving to do the Father's will. As tokens we bring and offer bread and wine, the offering of his body and blood. They constitute not only our continuing of the Son's offering of himself but also our offering of ourselves as contained therein.

The divine response to this is the releasing of the life and power of the Son for our good. This release of life and power we have seen as one of the essential elements of sacrifice and it is the aspect in which the Biblical doctrine of sacrifice comes nearest to the later doctrine of sacramental grace. The difficulty about the description of the Eucharist as a sacrament was that it was easy to infer that it was only a means of grace and nothing else.

I have spoken of the release of life and power, and these terms serve to give me a starting-point in my attempt to describe what is here involved, but the divine gift to us goes beyond these words and contains all that is needed for our welfare in the life in God. For example, it is important to include the gifts of understanding as well as of life and strength, a point in connexion with which we may recall the operation of the Spirit.

We have here to face an awkward question. We enact anew the Lord's Supper with bread and wine. We have seen that the words of administration in, for example, the Book of Common Prayer run as follows: 'The body (blood) of our Lord Jesus Christ which was given (shed) for thee, preserve thy body and soul to everlasting life.' We may easily be understood as saying that material things, body and blood, achieve for us spiritual ends, that we can, by means of matter, reach spiritual good.

We can go beyond this. We can regard the action of the Eucharist as a transaction with bread and wine and infer that this action, which is exclusively in the physical world, does achieve through bread and wine, or body and blood, all manner of results. In other words we may be held to be well on the road to magic.

Magic as a whole is not too easy to describe but we can detect certain kinds of magic. For example, there is the magic that consists in uttering the right words and doing the prescribed acts without more commitment than that. The performer controls both things and persons. All are subject to him provided he proceeds duly with word and deed.

It is easy to apply this to the Eucharist. If we enact the Eucharist according to the prescribed forms, we have before us the body and blood of the Lord and the ensuing release of his life and power. Suppose, however, we enact the form of the Eucharist but with a faulty intention, being faithless and impenitent.

There are two points about the consequences of this. The Old Testament analogy suggests that the sacrifice remains effective but that its consequences for the participants are disastrous. As we have seen, Paul in 1C. xi applies this to the Eucharist. It remains efficacious, but the consequences can be disastrous for the unworthy participant. Here the Eucharistic sacrifice retains its full force *ex opere operato*.

The second view is that for the unbelieving and the impenitent the whole transaction is null and void. It has no effect *per se* at all. There may be moral and spiritual consequences of taking part in the Eucharist in an unbelieving and impenitent state of mind. This may lead to hardening of heart and difficulty of repentance, but this could be the consequence of indulging in any forms in which we do not believe.

A consideration of the statement, 'This is my blood of the covenant' may help us here. With whom is the covenant made? Conceivably with the members of Christ's body as a whole, with the divine society, and not just with each group severally which re-enacts the Eucharist. The efficacy of the covenant rests accordingly on the reaction of the whole and not of any one section of it. Consequently, even if all who take part in any one celebration of the Eucharist are faithless or impenitent, this does not void the Eucharist itself.

We may take this further. In the story of Jacob at Bethel, God manifested himself as a God of promise and power, whether Jacob welcomed it or not. This is true of divine action as a whole. Its reality does not depend on human acceptance, though man may choose to accept or not.

We have then the promises of God. Where this is so, the efficacy of the action performed by man rests on such promises and not on any mechanical process, as is true in magic. We cannot make the existence of God or his activity conditional; it is also independent of magic.

Beyond this we have the fact of covenant. The covenant issues from God but affects both parties, God and man. By entering into the divine society and by participating in the resultant actions, man commits himself to the covenant proffered by God. It is in principle open to one of the contracting parties to take the initiative in establishing the covenant. In this connexion God is the initiator and our participation is a participation by way of response.

This contrasts with magic. Magic does not require a divine initiative. It acts by means of a mechanical procedure and all we have to know is how to work the machine. If its acts involve a god, it depersonalises and enslaves him. This is clear in many instances of ancient magic; a spirit who, at least sometimes, was formerly a god, becomes enslaved to anyone who knows how to work the mechanical process. A good example of this is to be seen in the *Testament of Solomon* and the related legends.

We can now distinguish between the divine initiators in the exchange between God and man, but we must return to our other problem: how do spiritual and material relate in this? My discussion of magic arose out of this, but in distinguishing between magic and the institution in which God and man meet we still have to answer our other question.

This question is created by the distinction between matter and spirit. The distinction is a useful one but, as has been implied early, is one which has only gradually developed. Greek philosophy and Biblical religion progressed in developing this distinction at different rates.

Let us take a concrete example, beliefs about the life after death. In Homer and the Old Testament the real *you* is the body, and death is the departure of vitality from the body. In Greek philosophy the real *you* is the soul, and death is the departure of the soul from the body. In the former view the real *you* identified with the physical body is apparently itself a material object, as can be seen most clearly from the verses at the beginning of the Iliad: 'And hurled to Hades many mighty spirits of heroes but the men themselves (αὐτοὺσ) it rendered to be a prey to the dogs and to all the birds' (Homer, *Iliad* i.3–5). Here αὐτοὺσ 'the men themselves' are the bodies in the battlefield which were devoured by dogs and birds.

In contrast to this is the picture in Plato's *Phaedo*, for example, where the ψυχή is sharply differentiated from the body and is immaterial and so intangible. This view established itself more and more firmly in subsequent centuries. The contrast between it and the Old Testament contributed something to the embarrassment of 1C. xv where Paul is trying to combine a belief in resurrection, which assumes that human existence is bodily existence, with this belief in the soul, or in this case spirit, πνεῦμα, as the centre of personality.

Be that as it may, already in antiquity the distinction had come to stay. We may today have modified it in various ways, but basically it is still with us and is assumed in a kind of modern Manicheism where 'physical' is bad and 'spiritual' is good.

With all its usefulness, this distinction leads us into difficulties once we assume that it is final. We are presented, in fact, with a belief in two worlds, which assumes some kind of relationship between them, but is not precise in stating what the nature of that relationship is. The spiritual and the physical do not come to terms with each other.

It is at this point that the institutions of the divine society make an important contribution. The association of bread and wine with the body and blood of Christ, and these again with the divine society, involves a series of equations which transcend the distinction between the material and the spiritual and point to a unity which lies beyond this distinction. This insistence on the unity of the world as a whole means that the distinction between material and spiritual is not final.

This has a significant consequence. The Manichean interpretation of the two constituents, spiritual and material, is no longer so plausible. Both can be good and can be used for good, both have their place in the holy world. The distinction between spiritual and material no longer coincides with the distinction between good and evil, and it becomes possible for us again to believe in the fundamental goodness of God's creation as a whole, just as we believe in its fundamental unity.

We can, of course, see other consequences of this unity. It becomes a supporting argument for the unity of Christ's body, the Church, and to that extent part of the theoretical basis for our attempts at reunion. It also conditions our approach to reunion in two ways.

First, it encourages us not to insist on uniformity. We have already seen two factors which make for variety, the spiritual–material and the good–

evil contrast. The relation between spiritual and material, good and evil, is constantly variable and makes for a considerable variety. Other factors add to this variety and even in redeemed mankind this variety persists. It must find itself at home in the divine society, but in such a way that the unity of the society, like the unity of God's creation, persists through our differences, is not overcome by them but transcends them.

This conclusion is important inasmuch as it has a bearing on another aspect of our experience. I have at various places in the course of my argument made use of the distinction between the holy and the profane. It can be very illuminating and at first sight might seem capable of consistent as well as rigorous application. We find however traces both among primitive peoples and in the Old Testament of inconsistency. Developments in the Old Testament sacrificial system tended to remove these inconsistencies and to apply the principles behind them more rigorously. Problems, however, were never completely solved, as we can see from the discussions of Rabbinic Judaism.

The drawing of hard-and-fast boundaries was never completed in the Christian Church. This can be seen from the empirical performance of the Church itself. It was the holy people of God, but in practice was capable of performances which can best be interpreted along Paul's lines as due to the presence of the old Adam and the new man together in the same person.

Likewise the Church lives in the two worlds. As we have seen, its part in the Eucharist is ambivalent. It enters into the holy world but it never leaves it, and we may say that there it properly belongs. Yet, if it is there, how can it enter? How can it return to where it always is?

Secondly, the Eucharist does not allow the variety to dominate, but maintains the basic unity already given in principle. We are concerned not just with establishing conditions according to which the diversities among us may live together in peace and goodwill, but with the reassembly of the body of Christ as the one divine society which mirrors on earth the divine unity.

We can see many other implications of the Eucharistic action when we reflect on it, but we must not so concentrate on the products and by-products of the Eucharist that we pay little attention to its central characteristic. As we have seen, it is an occasion of the meeting of God and man which has the distinctive character of focusing in itself the whole history of the exchanges between God and man. It would be strange if in doing all these things it failed to advance man's awareness of God.

This awareness of God first of all establishes our convictions about him. They become more deeply rooted in us and more certain as we renew this awareness. We may express this awareness in general terms, but we must know that it has particular application.

Let us take as an illustration of this our awareness of Christ as living. If we are aware of him in the Eucharist as alive, this does not commit us to all the details of bodily resurrection according to the New Testament, but it does commit us to the conviction that he not only is alive but has overcome death.

We may go further and say that our awareness of Christ in the Eucharist and what we learn about him in the tradition cohere, the two elements correcting and supplementing each other. We can see that each has something to contribute to this synthesis; we could not elicit from the awareness of Christ the details about him in the tradition: nor could the tradition itself automatically lead to the awareness of him that we have in the Eucharist. Each however helps the other to a greater knowledge of him.

What is true of Christ is true of God. Our awareness of him in the Eucharist coheres with what we learn of him in his dealings with man. Beyond the conditions of time and place we are taught something of his nature and thus something of his nature comes alive in our meeting with him.

If all proceeds as it should, we advance from enlightenment to enlightenment. It is here, much more than in any descent upon the elements of bread and wine, that we may see the work of the Spirit in the Eucharist. If we may trust Hippolytus, the Church is the society where the Spirit abounds (*Apostolic Tradition* xxxv). If this is true, we may hope to proceed not only from strength to strength, but also from knowledge to knowledge.

Two things characterise this process. First, it is open to all men whatever their gifts and, secondly, it demands from us all that we have. It is universal, but universally exacting.

If much is required from us, much is given. We receive all the riches of Christ, the goodness and love of God. They come to us in that awareness and are confirmed to us in manifestation after manifestation. In this the distinctiveness of the Eucharist lies not in our arriving among things we could not otherwise attain, but in its presenting to us, at one go, all that we can hope to receive in our life in God. All that holds good for the meeting of God and man is therefore focused and concentrated.

This may seem a difficulty, not only in the wealth of our experience of God in it, but also because it is described in a term which many must regard as unreal. Sacrifice in anything like its original form is, as we have seen in the first lecture, foreign language to us today. How can it be the significant term in our description of our Eucharistic experience?

Before we try to answer this question we must draw attention to one fact. 'Sacrifice' just as much as 'sacrament' is a term of Christian theology. It is part of one kind of contemporary technical language. It is a hard fact of experience that we cannot do without such language. This is true of any religion or religious movement. Even if it has little in the way of such language to start with, it soon develops a vocabulary to describe its distinctive tenets and practices. We can see this for example in the Group Movement mentioned earlier.

This modification does not, however, meet our principal difficulty. As we are using the word, 'sacrifice' describes a unique institution in Christianity. We claim to use it in a Biblical sense, but whereas, in the Bible, in the Ancient World and among many peoples today, sacrifice is practised in a variety of forms, the Eucharist is the sole surviving institution of this kind in Christianity.

As we might expect, the other significant example of sacrifice is the historic sacrifice of Christ. I have discussed the relation of this sacrifice to the Eucharist but, while we continually re-enact the Eucharist, Christ's historic sacrifice with all its relevance to us today is an event of the past which cannot be repeated.

Nonetheless Biblical sacrifice, including the sacrifice of Christ, provides valuable material in our attempt to describe sacrifice as a living institution, as distinct from a theoretical reconstruction. We may claim that in this way we arrive at an understanding of the Eucharist which is superior to other attempts at description. I have already argued this in the comparison of sacrament and sacrifice.

At this point we may try to answer another question: can we not find a more modern way of describing this institution? Sacrament in its day was such an attempt and we have seen that its weakness is its inadequacy. It concentrates on one aspect of the Eucharist. No amount of modernity will compensate for such inadequacy.

We can illustrate this in another direction. It is right that we should have liturgical revision. We need liturgy sufficiently in our terms for us to be able to use, but some liturgical revision is marked not only by modernity but also by impoverishment. Time and again the cry is raised that the old is better and we see on various sides dissident movements which sound like movements back to the past. Not all their supporters are from the ground up romantics of this kind. Their trouble is that they cannot bear the impoverishment that marks the new forms for them.

We would be hard put to it to find a contemporary term which is as adequate a description of the Eucharist as sacrifice, but suppose we have found such a term: are we any better off? We have spent much time and thought to this end and have only acquired another technical term.

One advantage sacrifice has. It can adjust itself to time and place. We saw hints of this in the Old Testament and we can see this happening in our time and circumstances. As an institution of the meeting of God and man, it is concerned not only with man as he was but with man as he is and shall be. In this way it has within itself the power to be modernised without losing any of its range of meaning. The institution is for all times and places.

This element of universality, of catholicity, has always marked the Eucharist, as it has marked the divine society which is the context of this sacrifice. It now exists in the hope of reaching its ideal limits. When it does so, the Eucharist will be found to be able to take in all mankind and all that redeemed mankind can do and offer in this exchange ordained by our Lord.

APPENDIX
A LITURGICAL DRAFT

The following text is intended to show how the view of the liturgy expressed in the lectures might be worked out in practice. It owes something to the liturgical texts in my book, *Remaking the Liturgy*, but it has been developed in certain directions. As is explained in it, there has been no drastic linguistic revision. I was concerned to concentrate the attention of the reader on the more narrowly liturgical features.

The text begins with the Kiss of Peace, as the migration into the Eucharistic action may be said to lie between the intercessions and the *pax*. The text of the Ordinary Preface has been retained because, though it might be strictly speaking held to be otiose, it does establish for the worshipper the context of the holy action.

It will be noted that the separation between the Institution Narrative and the Eucharistic action has been rigorously revived. The Narrative is present as one of the saving acts and is not the occasion of consecration. With the Kiss of Peace the worshipper enters the holy action, which begins with the taking of bread and wine.

It must be understood that the draft text is intended only as an example. Provided that the pattern and principle are preserved, variation is possible and to be expected.

THE KISS OF PEACE
Priest :　The peace of the Lord be with you always.
Answer :　And with thy spirit.

THE TAKING OF BREAD AND WINE
Here the Offertory or other anthem or hymn shall be sung or said while the gifts of those present are collected and brought to the altar. The altar shall next be made ready and the priest shall take bread and wine and place them upon it, mixing a little water with the wine. He shall then wash his hands. There shall be no singing when the bread and wine are taken and placed on the altar.

THE PRAYER OF THANKSGIVING
Priest :　Lift up your hearts.
Answer :　We lift them up unto the Lord.
Priest :　Let us give thanks unto our Lord God.
Answer :　It is meet and right so to do.
Priest :　It is very meet, right, and our bounden duty that we should at all times and in all places give thanks unto thee, O Lord, Holy Father, Almighty, Everlasting God, but chiefly are we bound to praise thee when we bring before thee this holy offering (*here the priest shall lay his hand on the bread and the wine*) of bread and wine. Therefore with Angels and

Archangels, and with all the company of Heaven, we laud and magnify thy glorious name; evermore praising thee, and saying:

Answer: Holy, holy, holy, Lord God of Hosts; Heaven and earth are full of thy glory. Glory be to thee, O Lord most High.

Priest: All glory and thanksgiving be to thee, almighty and everlasting God, for our creation, for thy sustaining goodness, and for thy covenants of mercy and peace to us and to all thy people.

Here particular thanksgivings shall be made.

We praise and bless thee for the redemption of the world by our Lord Jesus Christ: who became man to deliver all mankind from sin and death; in the Eternal Spirit he offered himself without spot to thee, O Father, and in the same night that he was delivered up he took bread, and when he had blessed thee, he broke it, and gave it to his disciples, saying: Take, eat, this is my body. Likewise after supper he took the cup, and when he had given thanks, he gave it to them, saying: Drink ye all of this: this is my blood of the Covenant which is shed for many. We proclaim his death and passion, his resurrection and ascension, the outpouring of his Spirit and the power of his Gospel, declared in all thy saints in thy holy Church, and we look for his coming again in glory.

All: Blessed is he that cometh in the name of the Lord. Hosanna in the highest.

Priest: We thank thee that thou hast called us to serve thee as a royal priesthood; we humbly beseech thee graciously to receive this our sacrifice of praise and thanksgiving, this bread and this cup which we offer according to his covenant, and to grant that we and all who partake thereof in faith may receive forgiveness of sins and all other benefits of his sacrifice, may continue true members of his body and be filled with his Spirit; and here we offer, O Lord, ourselves, our souls and bodies, to be in him a holy and living sacrifice unto thee, through the same thy Son Jesus Christ our Lord: by whom and with whom, in the unity of the Holy Ghost: all honour and glory be unto thee, O Father Almighty, world without end. Amen.

THE FRACTION

All the bread shall now be broken.

THE COMMUNION

Priest and congregation shall partake of the offering. The words of administration shall be:

Priest: The Body of our Lord Jesus Christ preserve thy body and soul unto everlasting life.

Answer: Amen.

Priest: The Blood of our Lord Jesus Christ preserve thy body and soul unto everlasting life.

Answer: Amen.

The bread and the chalice shall be given into the hands of those who partake.

INDEX OF BIBLICAL REFERENCES